MW01503918

A Time for Good News

Reflections on the
Gospel for
people on the go, Year C

Herbert O'Driscoll

Anglican Book Centre
Toronto, Canada

1991
Anglican Book Centre
600 Jarvis Street
Toronto, Ontario
Canada M4Y 2J6

Typesetting by Jay Tee Graphics Ltd.

Canadian Cataloguing in Publication Data

O'Driscoll, Herbert, 1928–
  A time for good news

ISBN 0-921846-41-X (Year C)

1. Bible. N.T. Gospels – Liturgical lessons, English
– Meditations. 2. Church year meditations. I. Title.

BS2565.O47   1991   226   C90-093340-2

For Moira and Colin
who made much possible

Contents

Suggestions for the use of this book

With this volume of short reflections on the Gospel passages of the lectionary's third year this trilogy comes logically and naturally to an end. I began this project to encourage people to take the Gospel into their own hands, especially if for some reason they could not be part of a worshipping community when it is being read. Sometimes we who have inherited a liturgical tradition of Christianity are a little apt to forget that we need not be entirely helpless when for some reason we cannot be part of the liturgy!

My original hope was that a book such as this might make it possible for anyone, wherever he or she might be, or however little time might seem to be available, to read the Sunday Gospel, then to read my simple and straightforward thoughts about it, and then, if there is a little time remaining, to think what these things might mean for their own living. If this pattern can become true for some then these pages will have served their purpose. However, there are many ways to put this book to good use. I suggest the following:

1 An individual worshipper could prepare for the Sunday liturgy by spending a few moments with the Gospel, either the evening before or on Sunday morning in a few quiet moments before the service.
2 The book could be taken on a weekend when one cannot be in a church but wants to be linked with the worshipping community by reading the same Gospel.
3 The book could be put in a briefcase on a business trip, in the door compartment of a car, or in the drawer of one's desk.
4 The book could be given as a small gift to people who are shut-in, either at home or in a nursing home, to link them week by week with the worshipping community.

5 The book could be given as a gift (perhaps by a parish) to each of its Sunday school teachers, who very often, by the service they render the church, are absent from the worshipping community during the Gospel reading and the homily.

6 These passages might be read by a lay person at a mid-week (or any) Eucharist as a short reflection on the Gospel. This offers yet another opportunity for involvement of worshippers in the liturgy.

7 A group of Sunday school teachers might take five minutes to share a page on the Gospel before teaching.

8 A Bible study group which wants to start its thinking and discussion, might find these pages useful once a week.

9 A prayer group might find ample focus for prayer in these short passages.

10 A vestry or church committee, even if the agenda is long, might consider these reflections short enough for an opening exercise.

11 A lunch-hour prayer or study group in a downtown office, a group of nurses or doctors in a hospital staff room, a group of teachers in a school — such groups, of which there are an ever-growing number in this time of spiritual searching, might consider these passages as starters.

A note about the sequence of the year in Christian time

All through the centuries of Christian faith there has been a unique sequence of seasonal time. It begins in early December with the first Sunday of Advent and ends in late November with the Sunday we now call the last Sunday after Pentecost, or the feast of the reign of Christ.

Each year is a little different because of the changing date of Easter, the joyous feast of Our Lord's resurrection. Sometimes the leader of a group, or an individual using this book, may want to check the sequence of the Christian year.

One could do this in various simple ways — perhaps by buying an inexpensive church diary or calendar, or by phoning a church office. The readings for Sundays are arranged in a three-year cycle; Year A always begins on the first Sunday of Advent in those years evenly divisible by three (1989, 1992, etc.). This book contains Gospel readings and reflections for Year C; books for Years A and B were published in 1989 and 1990 respectively.

Herbert O'Driscoll
Christ Church
Calgary
1991

First Sunday of Advent

²⁵"There will be signs in the sun, the moon, and the stars, and on the earth distress among nations confused by the roaring of the sea and the waves. ²⁶People will faint from fear and foreboding of what is coming upon the world, for the powers of the heavens will be shaken. ²⁷Then they will see 'the Son of Man coming in a cloud' with power and great glory. ²⁸Now when these things begin to take place, stand up and raise your heads, because your redemption is drawing near.'' ²⁹Then he told them a parable: ''Look at the fig tree and all the trees; ³⁰as soon as they sprout leaves you can see for yourselves and know that summer is already near. ³¹So also, when you see these things taking place, you know that the kingdom of God is near. ³²Truly I tell you, this generation will not pass away until all things have taken place. ³³Heaven and earth will pass away, but my words will not pass away. ³⁴Be on guard so that your hearts are not weighed down with dissipation and drunkenness and the worries of this life, and that day catch you unexpectedly, ³⁵like a trap. For it will come upon all who live on the face of the whole earth. ³⁶Be alert at all times, praying that you may have the strength to escape all these things that will take place, and to stand before the Son of Man.''

Luke 21:25–36

We live at a time when the Holy Spirit of God is calling us to involvement in the transformation of our world.

Ever since Jesus was a child in the synagogue school he would have known passages such as this one. We call it apocalyptic imagery. To feel your age of history is an apocalyptic age is to realize that it is a time of great threat but also of great promise. The reason why the passage seems very familiar to us is that we feel very much the same about our particular chapter of history as did Jesus' Jewish contemporaries about theirs. In fact we have only to read this passage and to reflect on it to realize how exactly it speaks to our situation.

"There shall be signs in the sun, and the moon, and the stars." Those were Our Lord's words two thousand years ago, but how true they are today. Our literature is full of books trying to pierce the mysteries of the universe. Are we the only creatures of this kind or are there millions of worlds where there is sentient life? We are trying to deal with the temptation to make space itself our new area of war! For us the heavens are a source of signs — of deep questions, hopes, doubts, fears, dreams.

"On the earth distress among nations." We have only to look around us to see that every country, all our human systems are under strain as we cross from the past into the future. Economic, educational, church and political systems, all are experiencing distress as they strive to serve our changing needs and our technological advances.

"Roaring of the sea and the waves." Most certainly we can hear that roaring. We know that we simply must change our ways as far as the rivers and lakes and oceans are concerned. Their roaring is the sound of their suffering under our treatment.

"People will faint from fear and foreboding." Our age knows only too well what the German word *angst* expresses, an all-pervading anxiety, unfocused because it is linked with almost everything. It is the feeling men and women have always had in an apocalyptic age.

"When these things begin to take place, stand up and raise your heads." Isn't that an unexpected thing for Jesus to say? Why does he say it? Because he is trying to get us to see that when all these phenomena surround us, the Spirit of God is involving us in the transformation of the world. That is the Good News for this week.

Second Sunday of Advent

[1]In the fifteenth year of the reign of Emperor Tiberius, when Pontius Pilate was governor of Judea, and Herod was ruler of Galilee, and his brother Philip ruler of the region of Ituraea and Trachonitis, and Lysanias ruler of Abilene, [2]during the high priesthood of Annas and Caiaphas, the word of God came to John son of Zechariah in the wilderness. [3]He went into all the region around the Jordan, proclaiming a baptism of repentance for the forgiveness of sins, [4]as it is written in the book of the words of the prophet Isaiah, ''The voice of one crying out in the wilderness: 'Prepare the way of the Lord, make his paths straight. [5]Every valley shall be filled, and every mountain and hill shall be made low, and the crooked shall be made straight, and the rough ways made smooth; [6]and all flesh shall see the salvation of God.' ''

Luke 3:1–6

Once again this Bible reading of Advent calls us to be involved in forming the future which God wills.

Very little happens in this passage; a person walks on to the scene and begins to speak. The reason Luke gives us this short scene is the significance of the person whom we meet and the significance of what he begins to say to the people of his own time and to us.

The person is John, a cousin of Jesus. He has been a member of a sect of Judaism called the Nazarites, who practised an intense and very ascetic faith, usually living in the desert. John had an outlook on the world of his day very like that of another sect called the Essenes. They lived in a desert community not far from where John began to preach. However, John differed from them in one very important way. The Essenes had left a society they were convinced was evil and condemned. John on the other hand called people to purify themselves as a preparation for being involved in the new kind of society he believed to be coming. To get across his message John echoed the prophet Isaiah, who had spoken to Israel centuries before when a wholly new future awaited their returning from exile to Jerusalem. John believed that a great change was coming again to Israel. God essentially was bringing that change about. Therefore John called men and women to offer themselves to God's service in bringing about the new age.

Does all this sound familiar to us to-day? It should, because there are many signs that we are a generation who is being asked by God to move through much change and danger and discovery to a new kind of society and a new chapter of history. If that is true, what can we learn from this passage?

The great lesson we Christians can learn from the genius of Judaism, and it is desperately important that we do, is that throughout their history, no matter what was happening, whether it was good or bad, joyous or terrible, successful or failing, the Jews always saw God at the heart of events. Let's try and apply this vision to our time. We are faced with immense change. In that change is not only immense threat and danger, but also tremendous possibility. The question haunting us all is How are we humans going to respond to this time, fearful as it sometimes is. A Christian has every motivation to respond with confidence and a sense of vocation. If God is at the heart of all that is happening, then we are called to nothing less than the formation of the future for God. That is the Good News for this week.

Third Sunday of Advent

[7]John said to the crowds that came out to be baptized by him, ''You brood of vipers! Who warned you to flee from the wrath to come? [8]Bear fruits worthy of repentance. Do not begin to say to yourselves, 'We have Abraham as our ancestor'; for I tell you, God is able from these stones to raise up children to Abraham. [9]Even now the ax is lying at the root of the trees; every tree therefore that does not bear good fruit is cut down and thrown into the fire.'' [10]And the crowds asked him, ''What then should we do?'' [11]In reply he said to them, ''Whoever has two coats must share with anyone who has none; and whoever has food must do likewise.'' [12]Even tax collectors came to be baptized, and they asked him, ''Teacher, what should we do?'' [13]He said to them, ''Collect no more than the amount prescribed for you.'' [14]Soldiers also asked him, ''And we, what should we do?'' He said to them, ''Do not extort money from anyone by threats or false accusation, and be satisfied with your wages.'' [15]As the people were filled with expectation, and all were questioning in their hearts concerning John, whether he might be the Messiah, [16]John answered all of them by saying, ''I baptize you with water; but one who is more powerful than I is coming; I am not worthy to untie the thong of his sandals. He will baptize you with the Holy Spirit and fire. [17]His winnowing fork is in his hand, to clear his threshing floor and to gather the wheat into his granary; but the chaff he will burn with unquenchable fire.'' [18]So, with many other exhortations, he proclaimed the good news to the people.

Luke 3:7–18

For a Christian the criterion for change in any new society must be Jesus Christ.

We are about to listen to a man who is convinced that an era has ended and a new and extremely challenging one is about to begin. Perhaps that is why John, whom people nicknamed "the baptizer," was so direct and almost brutal. To call your audience a bunch of snakes is not a promising beginning to an encounter! We can conclude only that John knew that he was up against a very thick and high wall of tradition. Perhaps he realized that all religion is capable of hardening into a wall that cannot hear a call to God's new purposes.

"The ax is lying at the root of the trees." It is a vivid image. John is saying that the changes are going to be radical. Nothing is going to stand merely because it is old or admired or a sacred cow! Unless it can prove its worth, i.e., "bear good fruit," it will be swept away. No group was immune because it had a long history or regarded itself as special, i.e., "have Abraham as our ancestor." The more we think about it the more we realize how chilling and how provoking it must have been to stand in that crowd, especially as a convinced traditionalist!

People began to ask John for specifics: "What then should we do?" John was very ready to answer each group with guidelines for their lives and their work. But when we look at the pattern of John's answers we see how he views the coming age. Essentially John sees a moral change.

If we ourselves are on the edge of a new chapter of history, what moral changes are we being called to? We are to choose a new relationship with the environment. We are to ensure that the genuinely weak and the poor in society are not betrayed, and to form new relationships between rich societies and poor societies. These tasks are just beginning.

As Christians let's not forget the last thing John says. Whatever the new society is going to be like it is going to reflect the character of Jesus Christ. He is the criterion for any Christian vision of a new society. That is the Good News for this week.

Fourth Sunday of Advent

[39]In those days Mary set out and went with haste to a Judean town in the hill country, [40]where she entered the house of Zechariah and greeted Elizabeth. [41]When Elizabeth heard Mary's greeting, the child leaped in her womb. And Elizabeth was filled with the Holy Spirit [42]and exclaimed with a loud cry, ''Blessed are you among women, and blessed is the fruit of your womb. [43]And why has this happened to me, that the mother of my Lord comes to me? [44]For as soon as I heard the sound of your greeting, the child in my womb leaped for joy. [45]And blessed is she who believed that there would be a fulfillment of what was spoken to her by the Lord.'' [46]And Mary said, ''My soul magnifies the Lord, and my spirit rejoices in God my Savior, [47]for he has looked with favor on the lowliness of his servant. [48]Surely, from now on all generations will call me blessed; [49]for the Mighty One has done great things for me, and holy is his name. [50]His mercy is for those who fear him from generation to generation. [51]He has shown strength with his arm; he has scattered the proud in the thoughts of their hearts. [52]He has brought down the powerful from their thrones, and lifted up the lowly; [53]he has filled the hungry with good things, and sent the rich away empty. [54]He has helped his servant Israel, in remembrance of his mercy, [55]according to the promise he made to our ancestors, to Abraham and to his descendants forever.''

Luke 1:39–55

Mary's ecstatic song teaches us that God uses the poor and the weak for God's transforming purposes.

Why did Mary decide to go to Elizabeth? We will never know for certain, but we can surmise Mary has just discovered that she is to bear a child. That is world-changing news in anyone's life. How does one grapple with that change? Maybe one chooses to find someone who will understand. For Mary there came the thought of Elizabeth. She too was expecting a child and, like Mary's, her child had been totally unexpected. Mary may have realized that her cousin was the one person she could talk to and have some chance of having the turmoil of her feelings understood. All of us know how wonderful it is to find that one person with whom we can talk and reveal ourselves.

For a moment let us apply that situation to ourselves. As Mary went on a journey with the child in her womb, so we go on the daily journey of our lives with Our Lord hidden in us. In the world we live in, confusing, challenging, exhausting, it is essential that we have someone with whom we can share our faith journey. That person may be an individual who has become a soul friend, or it may be a support group. It does not matter so long as we have one or the other. As Our Lord's mother needed a soul friend so do we.

"Blessed are you among women." Later that great statement was to become part of a universal prayer, but try to hear it as Mary might have heard it. Even if she totally believed and accepted her great vocation Mary would not have been human if she had not some questions and self-doubts and fears. If we look at Elizabeth's greeting we see something very important for those moments when someone turns to us in self-doubt and confusion. Notice how warmly and generously Elizabeth affirms Mary. By the time Elizabeth's loving affirmation is over Mary must have felt very different. How do we know? Look at her song. The lesson for us is that affirmation is the first great gift we can give to someone in a time of need.

Mary's song is something that will be sung down the ages. She sees in her own situation a great truth about God. Here she is, an unknown peasant girl, and God has seen fit to use her for ultimate greatness. Mary sees that it is the very nature of God to take that which is looked upon by the world as weak and poor and to make such things and such people the means of God's transforming work in the world. That is the Good News for this week.

Christmas

[1]In the beginning was the Word, and the Word was with God, and the Word was God. [2]He was in the beginning with God. [3]All things came into being through him, and without him not one thing came into being. What has come into being [4]in him was life, and the life was the light of all people. [5]The light shines in the darkness, and the darkness did not overcome it. [6]There was a man sent from God, whose name was John. [7]He came as a witness to testify to the light, so that all might believe through him. [8]He himself was not the light, but he came to testify to the light. [9]The true light, which enlightens everyone, was coming into the world. [10]He was in the world, and the world came into being through him; yet the world did not know him. [11]He came to what was his own, and his own people did not accept him. [12]But to all who received him, who believed in his name, he gave power to become children of God, [13]who were born, not of blood or of the will of the flesh or of the will of man, but of God. [14]And the Word became flesh and lived among us, and we have seen his glory, the glory as of a father's only son, full of grace and truth.

John 1:1–14

When we look at Jesus of Nazareth we are looking at a portrait of the nature of God. We are also being told that this same nature has touched our human nature.

One can imagine John's pen poised over the blank page in front of him. He probably knew the way those before him had started their versions of this extraordinary story. How could he do it justice? He decides to take us on a vast journey to the beginning of time and the heart of the universe. In modern idiom John begins at the Big Bang!

In images Graeco-Roman society could respond to John tells us that one of the oldest longings in the human mind has come true. Since the beginning of time there has been hidden at the heart of creation a secret word, a principle, a mystery. If we could encounter this word and discern its mystery we would know the truth at the heart of things.

This word is not merely a thing, an object. In fact it's not an ''it'' at all! This word is a living spirit, always in existence and always working as a kind of companion to God the creator. John tells us about this Word. He holds us out in the darkness of the universe and points to a light at the centre of all things. Then he tells us the unbelievable news that this Word has entered into the realm of creation we humans call home. This Word has actually entered into a body like ours and speaks to us in language we can understand. This Word, John tells us, has a human face and a human heart.

John Robinson, once Bishop of Woolwich, who became known all over the world for a little book he wrote while in hospital, ''Honest to God,'' once said that Jesus is the human face of God. It's a lovely and simple way to express a truth that is so wonderful we might well despair of ever finding words that are worthy of its wonder and its majesty. As so very often happens the simplest words do it best.

When you think about that statement — Jesus is the human face of God — you realize the wonder that follows. If Jesus is the human face of God, then the more we look at Jesus the more we see the nature of the ineffable mystery we call God. Even as I say this I am tempted to go on trying to find words to express all this. Far better that I should stop and let you do your own thinking and wondering about this Good News.

First Sunday after Christmas

⁴¹Now every year his parents went to Jerusalem for the festival of the Passover. ⁴²And when he was twelve years old, they went up as usual for the festival. ⁴³When the festival was ended and they started to return, the boy Jesus stayed behind in Jerusalem, but his parents did not know it. ⁴⁴Assuming that he was in the group of travelers, they went a day's journey. Then they started to look for him among their relatives and friends. ⁴⁵When they did not find him, they returned to Jerusalem to search for him. ⁴⁶After three days they found him in the temple, sitting among the teachers, listening to them and asking them questions. ⁴⁷And all who heard him were amazed at his understanding and his answers. ⁴⁸When his parents saw him they were astonished; and his mother said to him, "Child, why have you treated us like this? Look, your father and I have been searching for you in great anxiety." ⁴⁹He said to them, "Why were you searching for me? Did you not know that I must be in my Father's house?" ⁵⁰But they did not understand what he said to them. ⁵¹Then he went down with them and came to Nazareth, and was obedient to them. His mother treasured all these things in her heart. ⁵²And Jesus increased in wisdom and in years, and in divine and human favor.

Luke 2:41–52

We see Jesus in a moment of his development which is costly for family relationships. This humanity makes it possible for us to turn to him as Lord in such moments in our relationships.

Everyone of us must grow up, and it isn't easy. There can

be the thrill of discoveries, about oneself and about all sorts of things, but sometimes growing up can be painful, even frightening and hurtful. We can get hurt and we can hurt other people, sometimes the very people we love very much. Is that what we are seeing here in the early years of Jesus?

To be taken from the little town of Nazareth to the great city of Jerusalem must have been indescribably thrilling. Jerusalem was holy and unique in the lives of Mary and Joseph. It was a place of pilgrimage for any Jewish family who could possibly afford the journey, as well as a place of risks. It would be thrilling for a child because of its size and cosmopolitan nature. At the time of a feast its population exploded as people came in from all over the world for the religious festivities.

"Jesus stayed behind in Jerusalem." We tend to say that Jesus got lost; Luke doesn't say that. He suggests a decision on the boy's part, a decision that looks to be deliberate disobedience. This is probably a key moment in Jesus' development. He is asserting himself as a person. We speak nowadays of individualism. Is this not such a moment in the early years of Jesus?

To some of us that may sound presumptuous and irreverent. We are talking about Our Lord. But remember that the whole root and core of our faith is that Our Lord, whatever else he is, was fully human. What Christian faith says to me is that God knows what it means to be a human being! The way God knows this is that God lived a human life, and we encounter that life in Jesus of Nazareth. If that is true we cannot have it by halves. We can't have Jesus human in the parts we would like and not human in the parts we are not so sure about.

What we are seeing in this episode is Jesus looking for God, just as we did and do, and just as our children do in sometimes unlikely ways. What seems disobedience is obedience to a higher love and a higher parenthood. Mary and Joseph were frightened, hurt, and angry. As parents we understand that. What shines out of this passage is that Jesus had to do his growing as we have to. In doing so he hurt those whom he loved, as we do. It makes him even more a Saviour with whom we can share our humanity. It is the source of his forgiveness and his love. That is the Good News for this week.

Second Sunday after Christmas

¹In the beginning was the Word, and the Word was with God, and the Word was God. ²He was in the beginning with God. ³All things came into being through him, and without him not one thing came into being. What has come into being ⁴in him was life, and the life was the light of all people. ⁵The light shines in the darkness, and the darkness did not overcome it. ⁶There was a man sent from God, whose name was John. ⁷He came as a witness to testify to the light, so that all might believe through him. ⁸He himself was not the light, but he came to testify to the light. ⁹The true light, which enlightens everyone, was coming into the world. ¹⁰He was in the world, and the world came into being through him; yet the world did not know him. ¹¹He came to what was his own, and his own people did not accept him. ¹²But to all who received him, who believed in his name, he gave power to become children of God, ¹³who were born, not of blood or of the will of the flesh or of the will of man, but of God. ¹⁴And the Word became flesh and lived among us, and we have seen his glory, the glory as of a father's only son, full of grace and truth. ¹⁵(John testified to him and cried out, ''This was he of whom I said, 'He who comes after me ranks ahead of me because he was before me.' '') ¹⁶From his fullness we have all received, grace upon grace. ¹⁷The law indeed was given through Moses; grace and truth came through Jesus Christ. ¹⁸No one has ever seen God. It is God the only Son, who is close to the Father's heart, who has made him known.

John 1:1–18

The humanity we live out is a limited one; it is incomplete, even at its best and finest. In Jesus our humanity is taken into God and lived out among us in its ultimacy.

This passage was probably very familiar to you. We read it at Christmas. Rather, we read all but the last few verses, so today we concentrate on those four, hearing what they say to us.

Whenever I read this opening chapter of Saint John's Gospel, I always hear the great chords and harmonies of Richard Strauss's *Thus spake Zarathustra*. Millions of people became aware of this music when Stanley Kubrick used it to open the film *2001*. Kubrick used it to express the majesty of three of the great planets in our solar system in conjunction, and this is exactly the kind of vast panoramic vision which John reaches for in this passage.

John knows that what he has to tell us is so massive in its significance that there is really no language which will carry it adequately. Perhaps this is the reason why every word in his central statement is utterly simple and everyday. "The Word," he tells us, "became flesh and lived among us." God became our companion.

This companion is Jesus. If he is who John says he is, then Jesus is for us the source of all the spiritual energy we can ever need. In John's words, Jesus is for us "grace and truth." All our lives we receive from him whatever each and every aspect of our humanity needs. Jesus is prepared to be "grace upon grace" for us.

John says that we receive grace from what he calls Jesus' "fullness." What might this mean? It means, that for a Christian, Jesus is the ultimate our humanity is created to be. Paul is saying something like this to us when he says in his letter to the Ephesians that we are all called to "maturity, to the measure of the full stature of Christ." We live out an incomplete humanity, a partial one. Jesus is the real thing. That may sound cliché, but, as with the New Testament writers, sometimes the very simplest language does the job best, especially if you are trying to express a great mystery.

Just as this passage ends there is a beautiful statement we can easily miss. John says of Jesus that he ''is close to the Father's heart.'' I can think of no better prayer to close this short reflection than to offer this phrase as a prayer for both you and me, that there may be times in our experience when both of us know in our deepest being that we are close to the heart of God. That is the Good News for this week.

Epiphany

[1]In the time of King Herod, after Jesus was born in Bethlehem of Judea, wise men from the East came to Jerusalem, [2]asking, "Where is the child who has been born king of the Jews? For we observed his star at its rising, and have come to pay him homage." [3]When King Herod heard this, he was frightened, and all Jerusalem with him; [4]and calling together all the chief priests and scribes of the people, he inquired of them where the Messiah was to be born. [5]They told him, "In Bethlehem of Judea; for so it has been written by the prophet: [6]'And you, Bethlehem, in the land of Judah, are by no means least among the rulers of Judah; for from you shall come a ruler who is to shepherd my people Israel.'" [7]Then Herod secretly called for the wise men and learned from them the exact time when the star had appeared. [8]Then he sent them to Bethlehem, saying, "Go and search diligently for the child; and when you have found him, bring me word so that I may also go and pay him homage." [9]When they had heard the king, they set out; and there, ahead of them, went the star that they had seen at its rising, until it stopped over the place where the child was. [10]When they saw that the star had stopped, they were overwhelmed with joy. [11]On entering the house, they saw the child with Mary his mother; and they knelt down and paid him homage. Then, opening their treasure chests, they offered him gifts of gold, frankincense, and myrrh. [12]And having been warned in a dream not to return to Herod, they left for their own country by another road.

Matthew 2:1–12

All of us have gifts. Each of us chooses where to offer them. We can give them to the Old King of Death or to the Young Child of Life.

Even in the face of the gulf that has opened between the Bible and our culture millions of people know these images of the wise men on their camels coming to the Christ Child. When a religious story reaches out beyond the bounds of the community of faith and spreads into the general culture, one wants to ask questions. Why is it so powerful a story? Why are its images received so vividly?

If we look at the sequence of events and the characters, we may see a reason. But we must look at them, not just as particular characters, but as types of human beings. Initially, we notice that we have the Wise Men, the aging King Herod, and the newborn child Jesus. The wise men are searching for the newborn child. For them he is no ordinary child. They have travelled in search of a potential king. As far as Herod is concerned nothing could be more threatening. He has been king for a very long time and he realizes his hold on power is now very fragile. Hence, he is all the more determined to deal with any child who is being touted as king.

Now, instead of using names let us say only that we have the travellers or the searchers, the young child, and the old king. Immediately we see that we are talking about aspects of ourselves and of our world. Searching for the new, the new possibility, the new breakthrough, the new paradigm, is at the heart of our humanity. We search for the new within ourselves, within our institutions, within our world. In so far as we do this we are wise men and women. We are the travellers and the searchers.

The new can be seen in the young child, the image of all that God is bringing to birth in creation. To say this is not for a moment to diminish the reality and the specific significance of the birth of Jesus. We are for a moment putting on another lens to see another level of eternal truth in this story.

But hovering like a shadow over the quest of the travellers, and over the young child, is the old king. He has one objective: to stop the new birth, to kill the child. There is within each of us that which is trying to come to birth and that which is trying to prevent it. In our own lives, in the life of the church, of our country, and of every institution, the young child and the old king struggle.

What should we do? Well, what did the wise men do? They came to the young child and offered their gifts. For us the young child has a name. His name is Jesus. To offer our gifts to him is to acknowledge him as Our Lord.

The Baptism of the Lord or First Sunday after Epiphany

[15]As the people were filled with expectation, and all were questioning in their hearts concerning John, whether he might be the Messiah, [16]John answered all of them by saying, "I baptize you with water; but one who is more powerful than I is coming; I am not worthy to untie the thong of his sandals. He will baptize you with the Holy Spirit and fire. [17]His winnowing fork is in his hand, to clear his threshold floor and to gather the wheat into his granary; but the chaff he will burn with unquenchable fire." [21]Now when all the people were baptized, and when Jesus also had been baptized and was praying, the heaven was opened, [22]and the Holy Spirit descended upon him in bodily form like a dove. And a voice came from heaven, "You are my Son, the Beloved; with you I am well pleased."

Luke 3:15–17, 21–22

As John the Baptist speaks of one who is to come, we are shown the pattern of Our Lord's relationship with us.

"The people were filled with expectation, and all were questioning in their hearts." Doesn't that sound very like our own age? Expectation and great hopes for the future are tinged with many questions and doubts and fears. Although Christians aren't free from such fears, we believe that in Jesus Christ God entered our history. Christian faith does not give us a magic lens through which we can see the meaning and pattern of historical events, but it does assure us that they have a meaning and a purpose under God as the lord of history.

"I baptize you with water; but one who is more powerful than I is coming." Here is a truth in all our lives. Baptism is a symbol of our spiritual beginnings, but we are always being called farther and deeper in our understanding. Our spirituality is not fixed and static but growing. It is a journey where we must do a lot of changing and maturing. One who is more powerful spiritually than we can ever be is continually coming to us in various ways and calling us further.

"I am not worthy to untie the thong of his sandals." John the Baptist had no illusions about himself and his sentence speaks to us about ourselves. In the presence of Jesus you and I feel totally unworthy. We know only too well who and what we are. Yet we also know that without our deserving it in the least Jesus accepts us as friend and follower. This position of the Christian is immensely healthy spiritually and psychologically.

"His winnowing fork is in his hand." Here is where the loving and accepting relationship between us and Our Lord becomes something very sobering. We are responsible for our lives in the freedom Our Lord gives us to be totally ourselves. We are given Our Lord's love unconditionally, but having received it we are accountable to him. His gift to us is the grace of his love. Our gift to him is our faithful attempt, never entirely successful, to give him our deepest selves. That is the Good News for this week.

Second Sunday after Epiphany

¹On the third day there was a wedding in Cana of Galilee, and the mother of Jesus was there. ²Jesus and his disciples had also been invited to the wedding. ³When the wine gave out, the mother of Jesus said to him, "They have no wine." ⁴And Jesus said to her, "Woman, what concern is that to you and to me? My hour has not yet come." ⁵His mother said to the servants, "Do whatever he tells you." ⁶Now standing there were six stone water jars for the Jewish rites of purification, each holding twenty or thirty gallons. ⁷Jesus said to them, "Fill the jars with water." And they filled them up to the brim. ⁸He said to them, "Now draw some out, and take it to the chief steward." So they took it. ⁹When the steward tasted the water that had become wine, and did not know where it came from (though the servants who had drawn the water knew), the steward called the bridegroom ¹⁰and said to him, "Everyone serves the good wine first, and then the inferior wine after the guests have become drunk. But you have kept the good wine until now." ¹¹Jesus did this, the first of his signs, in Cana of Galilee, and revealed his glory; and his disciples believed in him.

John 2:1–11

The wedding at Cana can be a portrait of our lives: a lot of ordinary things are waiting to be changed by Our Lord's presence.

This passage introduces us to a wonderful, beautiful, and mysterious moment in the life of Our Lord. Perhaps it would be most helpful to see the wedding at Cana as a symbol of our own lives. After all a wedding is very much a symbol of life. Lives are joined; life and love are celebrated. Meetings take place, sometimes after many years; relationships are recovered, sometimes even begun. Families are bonded; new life is anticipated. A wedding is an immensely rich mixture. So let's look at the wedding in Cana as a symbol of life itself. If we do that, what follows?

"The wine gave out." At an eastern wedding that happening was a social catastrophe; it brought shame on the host and on the family. But, for us, what might it mean. There are times in all our lives when, in many senses, the wine gives out. If wine is celebration, joy, love, happiness, then we know only too well that for many reasons wine can run out. It can run out of relationships, either between men and women, or among friends, or among parents and children. Sometimes the wine of satisfaction with our job can run out. Life then can become meaningless and joyless.

At such times it becomes very important whether or not we have invited a certain guest to the wedding of life. John tells us that "Jesus was invited to the wedding"; we need to be sure that Our Lord's name is on our guest list! If it is, then we have someone to turn to when "the wine runs out."

"Jesus said. . . 'Fill the jars with water.'" Notice what Our Lord does. He doesn't tear off frantically looking for new wine, he turns to the supply of water that is already there. What is the water at the wedding of our lives? Perhaps it is the taken-for-granted things in our lives, the things we have always thought of as ordinary, everyday, run-of-the-mill. Our Lord suggests that we look at those things again. The ordinary person we are married to, the ordinary friends we have, the ordinary job we have, the ordinary life we lead. Jesus tells us to check out if by his grace they can be turned into wine, into more than the ordinary, into joy and satisfaction. That is the Good News for this week.

Third Sunday after Epiphany

14Then Jesus, filled with the power of the Spirit returned to Galilee and a report about him spread through all the surrounding country. 15He began to teach in their synagogues and was praised by everyone. 16When he came to Nazareth, where he had been brought up, he went to the synagogue on the sabbath day, as was his custom. He stood up to read, 17and the scroll of the prophet Isaiah was given to him. He unrolled the scroll and found the place where it was written: 18"The Spirit of the Lord is upon me, because he has anointed me to bring good news to the poor. He has sent me to proclaim release to the captives and recovery of sight to the blind, to let the oppressed go free, 19to proclaim the year of the Lord's favor." 20And he rolled up the scroll, gave it back to the attendant, and sat down. The eyes of all in the synagogue were fixed on him. 21Then he began to say to them, "Today this scripture has been fulfilled in your hearing."

Luke 4:14–21

Knowing that Our Lord spent time in the wilderness helps us to know Our Lord's presence in our personal wilderness.

"Jesus filled with the power of the Spirit returned to Galilee." The Gospel is telling us that it is from the wilderness that Jesus is returning. Why should this be significant? Because most of the time most of us think about life's wilderness experiences as negative.

What is a wilderness experience in life? First, let us think about the Judean wilderness. It is the setting for many events in the Bible — a lonely, frightening, and dangerous place. There are parts of human life which can be described in exactly the same terms. To feel that you are in a wilderness is to feel lost, threatened, and vulnerable. All of us know those feelings.

But why did Jesus choose such a place? Because he knew that there are times when we need to go apart and be solitary. Only then can we deal with certain things in our lives and become truly aware of what is going on inside us. Perhaps also he was aware of another deep truth about human nature. Sometimes all of us need to be challenged and tested. Here is the significance of Luke's telling us that Jesus returned from the wilderness "filled with the power of the spirit." For Jesus the wilderness experience was empowering, and that is exactly the lesson for us.

A wilderness experience in our lives can be empowering. However, we have to be honest. A wilderness episode in our lives can also break us. A marriage or any other relationship can hit a period of wilderness, so can a young person's life. We can hit a period of wilderness professionally. What makes the difference between empowering or breaking? For a Christian it can make a great difference to know that Jesus hit such a period, a time when he desperately sought answers as to how he should plan and act. Why is it a help to know this? Because then, when you and I hit our wilderness periods, we know that Our Lord knows how we feel. Then two wonderful things follow. The first is that we can be aware of his being with us in the wilderness. The second is that we can be utterly honest with Our Lord about the way we feel. We can acknowledge fear, anger, resentment, depression — everything. The simple fact is that a Christian need not feel alone in the wilderness. That is the Good News for this week.

The Presentation of our Lord Jesus Christ in the Temple

[22]When the time came for their purification according to the law of Moses, they brought him up to Jerusalem to present him to the Lord [23](as it is written in the law of the Lord, "Every firstborn male shall be designated as holy to the Lord"), [24]and they offered a sacrifice according to what is stated in the law of the Lord, "a pair of turtledoves or two young pigeons." [25]Now there was a man in Jerusalem whose name was Simeon; this man was righteous and devout, looking forward to the consolation of Israel, and the Holy Spirit rested on him. [26]It had been revealed to him by the Holy Spirit that he would not see death before he had seen the Lord's Messiah. [27]Guided by the Spirit, Simeon came into the temple; and when the parents brought in the child Jesus, to do for him what was customary under the law, [28]Simeon took him in his arms and praised God, saying, [29]"Master, now you are dismissing your servant in peace, according to your word; [30]for my eyes have seen your salvation, [31]which you have prepared in the presence of all peoples, [32]a light for revelation to the Gentiles and for glory to your people Israel." [33]And the child's father and mother were amazed at what was being said about him. [34]Then Simeon blessed them and said to his mother Mary, "This child is destined for the falling and the rising of many in Israel, and to be a sign that will be opposed [35]so that the inner thoughts of many will be revealed — and a sword will pierce your own soul too." [36]There was also a prophet, Anna the daughter of Phanuel, of the tribe of Asher. She was of a great age, having lived with her husband seven years after her marriage, [37]then as a widow to the age of eighty-four. She never left the temple but worshiped there with fasting and prayer night and day. [38]At that moment she came, and began to praise God and to speak about

the child to all who were looking for the redemption of Jerusalem. [39]When they had finished everything required by the law of the Lord, they returned to Galilee, to their own town of Nazareth. [40]The child grew and became strong, filled with wisdom; and the favor of God was upon him.

Luke 2:22–40

Jesus wishes to be the lord of our lives at every stage in our journey.

When we read that people had to be purified after childbirth we may wonder why? Did that long-ago society think childbirth was in some sense "dirty"? Far from it. Childbirth in Our Lord's society was cause for rejoicing and thanksgiving. It's the thanksgiving that is particularly important for us, because we can easily fall into taking it for granted.

Going for purification after giving birth meant that the whole process of birthing was offered to God. Thus, it was impossible to take that mysterious and dangerous process for granted. It also meant that the most earthy things of the body were brought into the realm of the spiritual. This concept can be a healthy corrective for late-twentieth-century folk. Our concepts of spirituality shy away from the physical all too easily, implying that it is not so holy as the spiritual. This tendency may be one of the reasons we have such trouble coming to terms with our physical nature.

Something very beautiful happens when Mary and Joseph take the child to the temple. Two elderly people, who presumably live there, arrive on the scene. They are Simeon and Anna, holy people, who are intensely interested in the child. Simeon asks to hold him. Despite a young mother's trepidation, Mary hands over the child.

As Simeon holds him the years seem to roll away. His shuffle becomes a bit of a dance, and his voice gets stronger as he sings a song of celebration. He sees great things ahead for this child. So does Anna when her turn comes. Then just as Simeon hands the child back he says something that changes everything. He looks at Mary and tells her that a sword shall pierce her heart because of her son.

What can this scene say to us? Notice first how every stage of life is represented. Jesus represents childhood, Mary youth, Joseph probably prime of life, Simeon and Anna old age. Yet all are centred on the Christ. When Christian faith can be like that it is at its richest. Of course it can't be true of every life. Some of us meet Our Lord at a later stage than others. But our simple prayer at this moment might be, that at whatever stage we encounter Our Lord and commit our lives to him, we may go on knowing him as lord of our life's journey. That is the Good News for this week.

Fourth Sunday after Epiphany

²¹Then he began to say to them, "Today this scripture has been fulfilled in your hearing." ²²All spoke well of him and were amazed at the gracious words that came from his mouth. They said, "Is this not Joseph's son?" ²³He said to them, "Doubtless you will quote to me this proverb, 'Doctor, cure yourself!' And you will say, 'Do here also in your hometown the things that we have heard you did at Capernaum.' " ²⁴And he said, "Truly I tell you, no prophet is accepted in the prophet's hometown. ²⁵But the truth is, there were many widows in Israel in the time of Elijah, when the heaven was shut up three years and six months, and there was a severe famine over all the land; ²⁶yet Elijah was sent to none of them except to a widow at Zarephath in Sidon. ²⁷There were also many lepers in Israel in the time of the prophet Elisha, and none of them was cleansed except Naaman the Syrian." ²⁸When they heard this, all in the synagogue were filled with rage. ²⁹They got up, drove him out of the town, and led him to the brow of the hill on which their town was built, so that they might hurl him off the cliff. ³⁰But he passed through the midst of them and went on his way.

Luke 4:21–30

A scripture passage which seems quite acceptable initially becomes explosive when Jesus applies it to the contemporary situation. This same transformation happens in today's church.

Jesus has just returned from the wilderness to his home town. Now he knows what he must do. He must put before people nothing less than a vision of a completely different way of living and a completely different kind of society. He is going to show what human life and society would be like if the reign of God were fully acknowledged. In other words, to use Martin Luther King Jr's great phrase, Jesus has a dream. The name he gives this dream is "the kingdom of God." Jesus now describes that kingdom by reading the great passage from Isaiah.

What is fascinating and ironic is that at first nothing happens. The great vision of a transformed society has been read but it has become the victim of its own familiarity. It has become a chant, a formula, a mantra. It's important to point this out because we do the same to scripture. We can listen to the most revolutionary scriptures and pass peacefully in worship to the next canticle!

Jesus knew this well. He does two things to break the familiarity. First, he says with devastating simplicity and directness, "Today this scripture is fulfilled in your hearing." At first that doesn't work. The stumbling block now is his own familiarity in the community. "Is not this Joseph's son," they murmur. But then Jesus touches a nationalistic nerve. He tells of two incidents where God has worked through outsiders, nonJews. God, Jesus is heard to be saying, is bigger than Judaism. In a moment he has his reaction. There is a near riot, and he barely manages to escape.

All long ago? By no means. Often in today's church when the great biblical visions of justice are read we accept them as magnificent scripture. As soon as a parallel situation is spoken of, some social injustice in our own or in another society, there frequently is anger. People remark that religion and politics don't mix. Protests are made that left-wing politics have no place in the pulpit, that only the Gospel should be preached!

Is it possible at such moments that Our Lord is asking us to recognize that God may be working in the world in political systems other than those we prefer? Is Jesus asking us to consider the possibility that we have a bigger God than we think? Why is it so important to consider? For the

same reason that it was important in that long-ago synagogue. The same Lord Jesus, risen, and our contemporary,
is asking us to consider the many voices of the world who
cry for justice. That is the Good News for this week.

Fifth Sunday after Epiphany

¹Once while Jesus was standing beside the lake of Gennesaret, and the crowd was pressing in on him to hear the word of God, ²he saw two boats there at the shore of the lake; the fishermen had gone out of them and were washing their nets. ³He got into one of the boats, the one belonging to Simon, and asked him to put out a little way from the shore. Then he sat down and taught the crowds from the boat. ⁴When he had finished speaking, he said to Simon, ''Put out into the deep water and let down your nets for a catch.'' ⁵Simon answered, ''Master, we have worked all night long but have caught nothing. Yet if you say so, I will let down the nets.'' ⁶When they had done this, they caught so many fish that their nets were beginning to break. ⁷So they signaled their partners in the other boat to come and help them. And they came and filled both boats, so that they began to sink. ⁸But when Simon Peter saw it, he fell down at Jesus' knees, saying, ''Go away from me, Lord, for I am a sinful man!'' ⁹For he and all who were with him were amazed at the catch of fish that they had taken; ¹⁰and so also were James and John, sons of Zebedee, who were partners with Simon. Then Jesus said to Simon, ''Do not be afraid; from now on you will be catching people.'' ¹¹When they had brought their boats to shore, they left everything and followed him.

Luke 5:1–11

If Jesus used Simon's boat, what ordinary and taken-for-granted elements of my life could he use?

As we watch Jesus move towards Simon's boat and climb into it we might ask ourselves What in my life could Our

Lord use? Are there things I may not think a great deal of, things I take for granted, which I could offer my Lord? Could he use some of my time? Some of my money? Some of my professional gifts? These things are to each of us what Simon's boat was to him.

"Put out into the deep water and let down your nets." Simon is nonplussed. They have just had a frustrating night: they didn't catch a thing. However, Simon pulls out into the lake, probably expecting to say "I told you so." What happens shakes him to the depths of his being. They are inundated with fish; so much so that they have to yell for help.

What would it mean for you and for me for Jesus to say to us "Put out into the deep and let down your nets?" He might be saying that he wants us to invest ourselves in areas where we are holding back. He might be saying that he wants us to invest more, risk more, contribute more to our marriage or our job or our children or our own spiritual journey. He might be suggesting that if we don't expect more we will certainly not find more!

Simon responds to the great catch by feeling unworthy. He has done nothing to deserve it. But, come to think of it, when we look at the various blessings we have been given, can we really say that we deserve them? If there is any truth in that thought, then perhaps it is time for us to bow down to Our Lord and acknowledge our unworthiness, as Peter did. Our Lord's great generosity and love toward us will fill us with a sense of gratitude, and will give us a sense of great joy. I know that this may sound too simple, yet the good news of Christ is essentially simple! Jesus said that unless we can be childlike, which surely includes simplicity, we can't even see his kingdom.

If Jesus said to his disciples "You will be catching men," and if we claim to be his disciples today, what can this promise mean for us? It will mean different things for each of us. But surely it means for all of us that we find some way of communicating to others that faith in Jesus Christ is an important factor in our lives. After all, if you or I discovered something of immense help to us, wouldn't we share it with others for whom we care? That is the Good News for this week.

Sixth Sunday after Epiphany or between 8 and 14 May

17He came down with them and stood on a level place, with a great crowd of his disciples and a great multitude of people from all Judea, Jerusalem, and the coast of Tyre and Sidon. 18They had come to hear him and to be healed of their diseases; and those who were troubled with unclean spirits were cured. 19And all in the crowd were trying to touch him, for power came out from him and healed all of them. 20Then he looked up at his disciples and said: ''Blessed are you who are poor for yours is the kingdom of God. 21Blessed are you who are hungry now, for you will be filled. Blessed are you who weep now, for you will laugh. 22Blessed are you when people hate you, and when they exclude you, revile you, and defame you on account of the Son of Man. 23Rejoice in that day and leap for joy, for surely your reward is great in heaven; for that is what their ancestors did to the prophets. 24But woe to you who are rich, for you have received your consolation. 25Woe to you who are full now, for you will be hungry. Woe to you who are laughing now, for you will mourn and weep. 26Woe to you when all speak well of you, for that is what their ancestors did to the false prophets.''

Luke 6:17–26

Our Lord is not only far above us but also beside us. He is judge and friend.

It's interesting that Luke says that Jesus ''came down with them and stood on a level place.'' Matthew, giving the same distillation of Jesus' teaching, said that ''When Jesus saw the crowds, he went up the mountain.''

Without making a big issue, what can we learn from this

interesting difference? All writers and artists impose something of themselves on their work; so it is with the Gospel writers. Matthew wants us to see Jesus as a second Moses giving a new vision and a new law. There needs then to be a mountain to parallel Mount Sinai. Luke's view of Jesus is different. For Luke Jesus is seen less as lawgiver and more as healer, teacher, friend. Luke's Jesus is accessible, a figure who is among rather than above others. That does not for a moment mean that, for Luke, Jesus is any less than he was for Matthew. We can be quite certain that there were many times when Jesus was remembered by his followers on the level among them and at other times on a sloping hillside where he would be above them. One writer chooses the former scene, the other the latter.

This difference in remembering could teach us about the differing modes of our own relationship with Jesus. All through history, in hymns and prayers, we try to define that relationship. Because it is so many faceted we end up choosing many images to express it. Jesus, we will say, is Friend. On the other hand he is Saviour. He is Child. He is also Judge. He is a Dying Man but he is also Our Risen Lord. In all these ways we are thinking of Jesus as either "among us on a level place" or above us "on the mountain." So Luke and Matthew are merely expressing the both/and quality of Our Lord which is there for all of us all the time.

Here we have a great spiritual insight not just an interesting idea. As a Christian I possess in Jesus Christ that which inspires me but also encourages me. Jesus calls me ever upward in my spiritual journey, calls me to strive to attain the heights on which my Lord stands, yet at the same time this same Jesus walks beside me as companion, accepting the fact that I cannot scale the great heights and will always have to spend a great deal of time on the lower slopes of spirituality, if not on the level plain!

One thing that might emerge from this short reflection is that differences in the Gospels can always give us some spiritual insight. That is the Good News for this week.

Seventh Sunday after Epiphany or between 15 and 21 May

[27]"But I say to you that listen, Love your enemies, do good to those who hate you, [28]bless those who curse you, pray for those who abuse you. [29]If anyone strikes you on the cheek, offer the other also; and from anyone who takes away your coat do not withhold even your shirt. [30]Give to everyone who begs from you; and if anyone takes away your goods, do not ask for them again. [31]Do to others as you would have them do to you. [32]If you love those who love you, what credit is that to you? For even sinners love those who love them. [33]If you do good to those who do good to you, what credit is that to you? For even sinners do the same. [34]If you lend to those from whom you hope to receive, what credit is that to you? Even sinners lend to sinners, to receive as much again. [35]But love your enemies, do good, and lend, expecting nothing in return. Your reward will be great, and you will be children of the Most High; for he is kind to the ungrateful and the wicked. [36]Be merciful, just as your Father is merciful. [37]Do not judge, and you will not be judged; do not condemn, and you will not be condemned. Forgive, and you will be forgiven; [38]give, and it will be given to you. A good measure, pressed down, shaken together, running over, will be put into your lap; for the measure you give will be the measure you get back."

Luke 6:27–38

Our Lord shares his vision of human behaviour totally obedient to God. We cannot live this vision but it will be light and grace to us for ever.

We are listening to the heart of Our Lord's public ministry. Every word of this passage, and of what comes before and after it in this chapter, will be relevant for human life for all time. Here Jesus communicates a vision of human life and human relationships which challenges all our normal levels of acceptance.

"Love your enemies, do good . . . bless . . . pray for those who abuse you." This whole passage stands like a mountain peak in the moral and ethical imagination of humanity. It is a statement of the ultimate: it is not possible to reach above or beyond it. Perhaps that is why he repeats the challenge in image after image. Loving, doing good, blessing, praying, offering the other cheek, offering one's shirt, responding to begging, — each one of these images repeats the demand for the ultimate moral response not merely to friend but also to enemy, to the attacker, the abuser, the thief.

Can you and I respond to this demand? Both of us are quite safe in saying No! Then why does this seemingly impossible demand haunt us. Why does it continue to shine like a light in all the darkness of human experience? For two reasons. Jesus did not just say these things to us; he lived them among us. To give oneself totally? He did. To pray for those who abuse us? He did. To love one's enemies? He did. This is why this passage can never be dismissed as idle dreaming for human life. We cannot dismiss something as unreal and visionary if it becomes real in front of our eyes and walks among us as Jesus did.

The second reason this vision of human response will not go away is that there is something in us that responds to it even if we cannot reach its ultimate heights. That something is perhaps the most wonderful and valuable element in our human nature. Saint John once spoke of it as ''the

light that lighteneth every man that cometh into the world.''
It is a light that, though it can be brought very low by our
own will and our own self, can never be extinguished. It
is this lesser light in our lives which reaches out for the
greater light which is Christ. His light blinds us but we are
attracted to it like a plant bending towards the light. As
Isaiah said centuries before Our Lord, ''The people who
walk in darkness have seen a great light.'' Who are these
people? We are. That is the Good News for this week.

Eighth Sunday after Epiphany or between 22 and 28 May

[39]He also told them a parable. "Can a blind person guide a blind person? Will not both fall into a pit? [40]A disciple is not above the teacher, but everyone who is fully qualified will be like the teacher. [41]Why do you see the speck in your neighbor's eye, but do not notice the log in your own eye? [42]Or how can you say to your neighbor, 'Friend,' let me take out the speck in your eye, when you yourself do not see the log in your own eye? You hypocrite, first take the log out of your own eye, and then you will see clearly to take the speck out of your neighbor's eye. [43]No good tree bears bad fruit, nor again does a bad tree bear good fruit; [44]for each tree is known by its own fruit. Figs are not gathered from thorns, nor are grapes picked from a bramble bush. [45]The good person out of the good treasure of the heart produces good, and the evil person out of evil treasure produces evil; for it is out of the abundance of the heart that the mouth speaks. [46]Why do you call me 'Lord, Lord,' and do not do what I tell you? [47]I will show you what someone is like who comes to me, hears my words, and acts on them. [48]That one is like a man building a house, who dug deeply and laid the foundation on rock; when a flood arose, the river burst against that house but could not shake it, because it had been well built. [49]But the one who hears and does not act is like a man who built a house on the ground without a foundation. When the river burst against it, immediately it fell, and great was the ruin of that house."

Luke 6:39–49

A life firmly founded on faith in Jesus Christ can remain strong when other foundations disintegrate.

As we move through a passage like this one, we need to remember that it is a synopsis of Our Lord's teaching. The disconnected sayings, almost proverbs, found here, he may well have talked about on different occasions and sometimes at greater length.

"Can a blind person lead a blind person?" If we are going to be of any use to one another spiritually we cannot merely indulge in religious information and clever argument. We ourselves need to have some experience of a spiritual journey towards and with Our Lord before we can help someone else on that journey.

"Why do you seek the speck in your neighbour's eye?" Why does a certain trait in someone else make us angry or want to condemn or reject them? Because all too often that very same trait is in us, perhaps pushed down into our unconscious and never fully acknowledged. Without realizing it we project on to someone else our dislike of its presence in ourselves. In other words we do not notice "the log in (our) own eye."

"Good tree . . . bad tree . . . good person . . . evil person." Again Jesus drives home a single thought by repeated images. The insight is that the ultimate test of our promises and statements is our performance.

"A man building a house." In a spiritual sense all of us are doing just this. Jesus tells of two people who built houses. The implication is that the two houses look much the same. It is only when the foundation is checked that a fundamental difference appears. One is built on rock and the other on sand. When a flood comes to test both foundations one house stands and the other falls.

You and I can build the house of our life on many kinds of foundations. In fact, we can sometimes build rather magnificent houses, a magnificent lifestyle, a charming personality, a hospitable stance, involvement in the community, generosity to causes, and so on. Nothing about these things is other than desirable and praiseworthy. The question always in each of our lives is about who and what we are behind all the appearance of our lives. What is the real person based on? What foundation is our life built on? Christian faith tells us that if a life is founded on faith in Jesus Christ then that life can survive when other foundations disintegrate. That is the Good News for this week.

Ninth Sunday after Epiphany or between 29 May and 4 June

[1]After Jesus had finished all his sayings in the hearing of the people, he entered Capernaum. [2]A centurion there had a slave whom he valued highly, and who was ill and close to death. [3]When he heard about Jesus, he sent some Jewish elders to him, asking him to come and heal his slave. [4]When they came to Jesus, they appealed to him earnestly, saying, "He is worthy of having you do this for him, [5]for he loves our people, and it is he who built our synagogue for us." [6]And Jesus went with them, but when he was not far from the house, the centurion sent friends to say to him, "Lord, do not trouble yourself, for I am not worthy to have you come under my roof; [7]therefore I did not presume to come to you. But only speak the word, and let my servant be healed. [8]For I also am a man set under authority, with soldiers under me; and I say to one, 'Go,' and he goes, and to another, 'Come,' and he comes, and to my slave, 'Do this,' and the slave does it." [9]When Jesus heard this he was amazed at him, and turning to the crowd that followed him, he said, "I tell you, not even in Israel have I found such faith." [10]When those who had been sent returned to the house, they found the slave in good health.

Luke 7:1–10

We make many assumptions about people who seem outside our particular world. Sometimes our stereotypes can be challenged.

Why does Luke include this particular healing in his recalling of Our Lord's ministry? One can't help thinking that the reason lies in the identity and the occupation of the man who asks for help. Before we look at anything else let's look at a single sentence of Our Lord and see what we learn from it. Luke tells us that Jesus marvelled at this Roman noncommissioned officer. Our Lord said "I tell you, not even in Israel have I found such faith."

Why was Jesus surprised at this man's attitude? Perhaps because the man was not Jewish but Roman. To put it mildly he was an outsider in that world of Galilee on the edge of empire. After all, he embodied the much resented Roman occupation forces. But then we are all tempted to make assumptions about those who seem to us to be outsiders to our world. Mostly those assumptions are negative, and we should guard against them very carefully. A related attitude is the assumption that even other forms of Christianity are not so faithful as our own. We make great blanket statements about another Christian tradition, especially if it happens to be wrestling with some painful and complex issue which we do not happen to be facing at the same time. We forget that within that other tradition, feeling its pain and striving to be faithful and Christlike, are some of the finest Christian men and women we could ever meet. Christlike spirituality has no limitations geographically or institutionally. To our astonishment we can discover it in the most unexpected people, sometimes in people whom we have blithely written off.

Yet another surprise God gives us from time to time is our discovery of a Christlikeness in someone who doesn't seem to know or care that Christ even exists! They may even delight in challenging our Christian claims, while all the time it will be very obvious to us that in their integrity and sensitivity and loving actions they already possess his spirit in the heart, maybe, perish the thought, to a greater extent than we ourselves!

All these thoughts come to mind as we see Jesus say a fervent Yes to this centurion's plea. Graciously and generously Jesus gives himself to this hitherto outsider. This of course transforms the relationship so that there is no longer a question of outsider and insider. By this action Our Lord heals not only disease but relationships. We have it in our power much more often than we realize to heal relationships. That is the Good News for this week.

First Sunday in Lent

[1]Jesus, full of the Holy Spirit, returned from the Jordan and was led by the Spirit in the wilderness, [2]where for forty days he was tempted by the devil. He ate nothing at all during those days, and when they were over, he was famished. [3]The devil said to him, "If you are the Son of God, command this stone to become a loaf of bread." [4]Jesus answered him, "It is written, 'One does not live by bread alone.' " [5]Then the devil led him up and showed him in an instant all the kingdoms of the world. [6]And the devil said to him, "To you I will give their glory and all this authority; for it has been given over to me, and I give it to anyone I please. [7]If you, then, will worship me, it will all be yours." [8]Jesus answered him, "It is written, 'Worship the Lord your God, and serve only him.' " [9]Then the devil took him to Jerusalem, and placed him on the pinnacle of the temple, saying to him, "If you are the Son of God, throw yourself down from here, [10]for it is written, 'He will command his angels concerning you, to protect you,' [11]and 'On their hands they will bear you up, so that you will not dash your foot against a stone.' " [12]Jesus answered him, "It is said, 'Do not put the Lord your God to the test.' " [13]When the devil had finished every test, he departed from him until an opportune time.

Luke 4:1–13

From Our Lord's testing we learn to examine all our motivations. Do we do what we do merely to satisfy our egos?

Jesus has made the decision that will affect all history. He has decided to move out of Nazareth into public ministry. He has just undergone baptism and has had a shattering experience of the presence of God in which both he and his intentions are deeply affirmed. He now must take the next step.

It is one thing to make a big decision. It is often quite another to put the big decision into action. That is what Jesus has to do. He is "filled with the power of the Spirit," but what does that Spirit want him to do? He goes into the desert to work that out. There he faces the demons that face us all when we must wrestle with choices that are life-changing. Sometimes the call of God to go in a certain direction may be very strong, but we may still have a great deal of agonizing about the specific steps. The temptations or tests in the wilderness are Jesus' wrestling with alternatives.

Presumably when he returned Jesus told of his wilderness experience in the same vivid images he tells other things. If we look at the tests we see a pattern. Each time, the test is a temptation to get people to follow him by certain devices. The first is that he bribe people, the second is that he impress people, and the third that he dominate them. To all of these Jesus says a resounding No. Why? Because he sees that he is being drawn by the temptation to satisfy his own ego. It is also the temptation to power at any price and by any means. Jesus dismisses the possibility and then makes his decision. In this passage we are not told that decision but the first things Jesus does after returning tell us clearly what he has decided to do. He calls his first four disciples.

This action tells us that Jesus decided to go the way of slow, undramatic building of a community of faith, doing it at a pace where he could really know those whom he called. More and more in today's church we are being called to do that. But we are taught something else by Our Lord's time of temptation. We are taught to examine the motivations for all our plans and actions. By his example Our Lord asks us whether our intentions are as we like to think, or only satisfying our own egos? That is the Good News for this week.

Second Sunday in Lent

[31]At that very hour some Pharisees came and said to him, "Get away from here, for Herod wants to kill you." [32]He said to them, "Go and tell that fox for me, 'Listen, I am casting out demons and performing cures today and tomorrow, and on the third day I finish my work. [33]Yet today, tomorrow, and the next day I must be on my way, because it is impossible for a prophet to be killed outside of Jerusalem.' [34]Jerusalem, Jerusalem, the city that kills the prophets and stones those who are sent to it! How often have I desired to gather your children together as a hen gathers her brood under her wings, and you were not willing! [35]See, your house is left to you. And I tell you, you will not see me until the time comes when you say, 'Blessed is the one who comes in the name of the Lord.' "

Luke 13:31–35

Jesus felt all the tensions and pressures that we know so well. This insight into the Gospel makes him even more a loving Saviour.

It is these rich moments in the Gospel that help dispel the notion that Our Lord's life was free of all the problems that plague us daily. As we look at Our Lord portrayed in such things as stained glass windows, it is easy to think of his life as constant serenity. That Jesus is always in charge, never bothered, never tense. But here we encounter a passage where Our Lord's humanity comes through.

"Some Pharisees came and said to him, 'Get away . . . Herod wants to kill you.' " Here are the Pharisees, whom we are apt to brand immediately as Our Lord's enemies, warning him about his safety. There must have been some very fine men and women among the Pharisees, and there were undoubtedly some who were drawn to the Galilean rabbi. The simple but important lesson is that we should always watch the temptation to stereotype people. Saying that a whole class or nationality are such and such is invariably proved wrong, yet we go on doing it. People who have a different way of expressing their Christian faith can all too easily be swept into one category for our neat condemnation.

"Go and tell that fox," Jesus replies scathingly and dismissively. He has nothing but contempt for him. Then sarcastically Our Lord says "it is impossible for a prophet to be killed outside of Jerusalem." He is suggesting that Jerusalem has a long history of lashing out at anyone who tries to talk to its entrenched conservatism. Jesus then begins a sad and grim reflection on his own relationship with Jerusalem. He expresses all that he has passionately wished for only to have it thrown back in his face.

Notice Jesus' rapid changes of mood. First there is anger, then sarcasm, then sadness. Some quick changes in you and me would indicate extreme emotional pressure and lack of control of our responses. There is no reason not to think this of Jesus. Once again it is important to point out that a passage like this performs the invaluable function of showing Our Lord's genuine humanity. When we are under pressure, when we are far from being in charge, we can silently say in prayer "Lord, you know these things. You have been where I am now. Help me." To realize that such a prayer is possible can be immense grace to a Christian. That is the Good News for this week.

Third Sunday in Lent

[1]At that very time there were some present who told him about the Galileans whose blood Pilate had mingled with their sacrifices. [2]He asked them, "Do you think that because these Galileans suffered in this way they were worse sinners than all other Galileans? [3]No, I tell you; but unless you repent, you will all perish as they did. [4]Or those eighteen who were killed when the tower of Siloam fell on them — do you think that they were worse offenders than all the others living in Jerusalem? [5]No, I tell you; but unless you repent, you will all perish just as they did." [6]Then he told this parable "A man had a fig tree planted in his vineyard; and he came looking for fruit on it and found none. [7]So he said to the gardener, 'See here! For three years I have come looking for fruit on this fig tree, and still I find none. Cut it down! Why should it be wasting the soil?' [8]He replied, 'Sir, let it alone for one more year, until I dig around it and put manure on it. [9]If it bears fruit next year, well and good; but if not, you can cut it down.'"

Luke 13:1–9

God offers us a relationship which we are free to accept or reject. He will give us every chance to respond.

As in any city news travelled fast in Jerusalem. In this passage we get a glimpse into the events of that particular society, the equivalent of our television news. Everyone would have been aware of these happenings and would have had various reactions. Events, especially dramatic and shocking events, force us to deal with our emotional reaction. For us it may be a tragedy in a neighbour's or friend's family, a plane crash half way across the world. It makes us begin to think about our own lives and the meaning of life itself with its mixture of triumphs and tragedies.

One event in Jerusalem was a particularly vicious, not to mention politically unwise, decision of the Procurator to execute certain Jews who challenged his demands. The second was what we would today probably call an industrial accident. A building collapsed killing eighteen people. Jesus takes these two events and uses them to make a point. He questions a perennial human reaction to tragedy. Did it happen to certain people because they somehow deserved it? Is God that kind of God? Jesus says a resounding No. Accidents are accidents; acts of aggression are acts of aggression. Those affected by either are not the victims of a punishing God.

Jesus then adds a warning. While emphasizing that there is no link between tragedy and any guilt in those affected, he points out that we can never escape the fact that there are consequences to all our decisions and actions — sometimes very sad and even tragic consequences that we never intended.

Jesus adds a parable. A man checks a fig tree for figs and finds there are none. There have been none for three years, so he decides to cut the tree down. It is a frequent theme of Our Lord. Our lives, he tells us again and again, are accountable. We are responsible beings who are judged by the fruits of our lives. Then the parable gives us a glimpse of a merciful love which will give this tree more nourishment, more tending. So will a merciful God respond to any possibility of response in us. But Our Lord has a warning. For the tree there is one more year. For us there comes a time when God allows us the freedom of our own choice not to respond. Sadly but inevitably a relationship ends. That is the Good News — cautionary but still good — for this week.

Fourth Sunday in Lent

[1]Now all the tax collectors and sinners were coming near to listen to him. [2]And the Pharisees and the scribes were grumbling and saying, ''This fellow welcomes sinners and eats with them.'' [3]So he told them this parable: [11]Then Jesus said, ''There was a man who had two sons. [12]The younger of them said to his father, 'Father, give me the share of the property that will belong to me.' So he divided his property between them. [13]A few days later the younger son gathered all he had and traveled to a distant country, and there he squandered his property in dissolute living. [14]When he had spent everything, a severe famine took place throughout that country, and he began to be in need. [15]So he went and hired himself out to one of the citizens of that country, who sent him to his fields to feed the pigs. [16]He would gladly have filled himself with the pods that the pigs were eating; and no one gave him anything. [17]But when he came to himself he said, 'How many of my father's hired hands have bread enough and to spare, but here I am dying of hunger! [18]I will get up and go to my father, and I will say to him, ''Father, I have sinned against heaven and before you; [19]I am no longer worthy to be called your son; treat me like one of your hired hands.'' ' [20]So he set off and went to his father. But while he was still far off, his father saw him and was filled with compassion; he ran and put his arms around him and kissed him. [21]Then the son said to him, 'Father, I have sinned against heaven and before you; I am no longer worthy to be called your son.' [22]But the father said to his slaves, 'Quickly, bring out a robe — the best one — and put it on him; put a ring on his finger and sandals on his feet. [23]And get the fatted calf and kill it, and let us eat and celebrate; [24]for this son of mine was dead and is alive again; he was lost and is found!' And

they began to celebrate. ²⁵Now his elder son was in the field; and when he came and approached the house, he heard music and dancing. ²⁶He called one of the slaves and asked what was going on. ²⁷He replied, 'Your brother has come, and your father has killed the fatted calf, because he has got him back safe and sound.' ²⁸Then he became angry and refused to go in. His father came out and began to plead with him. ²⁹But he answered his father, 'Listen! For all these years I have been working like a slave for you, and I have never disobeyed your command; yet you have never given me even a young goat so that I might celebrate with my friends. ³⁰But when this son of yours came back, who has devoured your property with prostitutes, you killed the fatted calf for him!' ³¹Then the father said to him, 'Son, you are always with me, and all that is mine is yours. ³²But we had to celebrate and rejoice, because this brother of yours was dead and has come to life; he was lost and has been found.' ' ''

Luke 15:1–3, 11–32

In the relationships between a father and his two sons we glimpse the glory of the love of God which welcomes all of us home, however and wherever we have wandered.

It is ironic that this parable of Our Lord became known as the parable of the prodigal son; its scope is far wider. It is so rich in insights about the way we human beings function and relate that in these few lines we cannot possibly exhaust its spiritual insight.

First, we see that there are two distinct chapters and three characters. The first chapter is about the younger son, the second about the older. Each chapter describes the relationship of each son to his father and, in a lesser sense, to one another.

Very quickly Jesus draws an unflattering portrait of the

younger son. He is self-centred, uncaring, ungrateful, and he experiences the consequences of his choices. But then there come the great words "when he came to himself." This is the point of turning and returning. He comes home and is received by his welcoming father with great joy. Seeing the welcome, the older son is incapable of understanding the dynamic of what is happening, because the experience is an unknown for him. He, the very person who has by his own claim always retained the relationship with his father, now spurns it. The younger son who had spurned it, now knows its value and claims it. The older son has never felt the need of forgiveness and so cannot understand what it means to be forgiven. Tragically and paradoxically, by his never leaving home he cannot know the joy of returning, by his never having stepped away from a relationship he cannot step back towards it and be received, by his never becoming a person in his own right he cannot understand either the pain and cost of doing that, knowing that one has hurt others in the process, or the joy of coming to know that one's hurtful action has been forgiven.

Tennyson once said that "it is better to have loved and lost than never to have loved at all." In this great story we see a similar insight into human nature and human relationships. It is better, Jesus is saying, to discover our true self, even at the cost of personal pain and hurt to those who love us, than never to discover our true self at all. We must add one most important point. All is made possible by the capacity of the father to love and forgive. As we say this, we must never forget that in telling us this story Our Lord is showing us the very nature of God. In that eternal love lies the possibility for us all of returning to the loves and lives which in our various ways we have abandoned, hurt, and betrayed, sometimes unknowingly. That is the Good News for this week.

Fifth Sunday in Lent

¹Six days before the Passover Jesus came to Bethany, the home of Lazarus, whom he had raised from the dead. ²There they gave a dinner for him. Martha served, and Lazarus was one of those at the table with him. ³Mary took a pound of costly perfume made of pure nard, anointed Jesus' feet, and wiped them with her hair. The house was filled with the fragrance of the perfume. ⁴But Judas Iscariot, one of his disciples (the one who was about to betray him), said, ⁵"Why was this perfume not sold for three hundred denarii and the money given to the poor?" ⁶(He said this not because he cared about the poor, but because he was a thief; he kept the common purse and used to steal what was put into it.) ⁷Jesus said, "Leave her alone. She bought it so that she might keep it for the day of my burial. ⁸You always have the poor with you, but you do not always have me."

John 12:1–8

To look at Our Lord is to realize our spiritual poverty, yet to realize this is to be spiritually rich.

Bethany is very near to Jerusalem, just to the east. Here lived the three people whom we could say more than any other were friends of Jesus. Their house was obviously open to Jesus and he seems to have appreciated that. We have no record of his ever having spent a night in Jerusalem and we can only surmise that it was here with Mary, Martha, and Lazarus that he spent time when he was in the vicinity of the city. Their relationship shows us another aspect of the humanity of Our Lord in that he, like us, needed friends among whom he could be completely himself, acknowledging weariness or despondency or anything else.

"They gave a dinner for him. Martha served." What is amusing here and very typical of human nature is that things have changed very little despite Martha's remonstration about Mary's not helping her. Martha still serves! Our roles do not change overnight in any family.

"Mary took a pound of costly perfume." Here is one of the mysteries of the Gospels: Who exactly was the person who made this moving and passionate gesture? The gesture is mentioned differently by every Gospel writer. Matthew and Mark recall it happening in another house in Bethany. Luke recalls it happening at a dinner in a rich house in Jerusalem. There the woman is "a sinner." John places the incident in the Lazarus house and says Mary is the woman. What we can do however is place ourselves in that long-ago moment and ask what it would mean for us to give something extremely precious from our own lives to Our Lord.

"You always have the poor with you." It's a haunting statement and it has been used for many purposes throughout history. It is a judgement on all social systems in history, and on our own spiritual lives. Whoever we are, whatever our gifts may be, whatever our prominence in society or our wealth, we will be poor in certain areas of our lives. Particularly when we place ourselves beside Our Lord we will realize that, as Isaiah once said, our righteousness is as rags. Paradoxically, to realize our spiritual poverty is to become spiritually rich. That is the Good News for this week.

Sunday of the Passion
With the Liturgy of the Palms

[14]When the hour came, he took his place at the table, and the apostles with him. [15]He said to them, "I have eagerly desired to eat this Passover with you before I suffer; [16]for I tell you, I will not eat it until it is fulfilled in the kingdom of God." [17]Then he took a cup, and after giving thanks he said, "Take this and divide it among yourselves; [18]for I tell you that from now on I will not drink of the fruit of the vine until the kingdom of God comes." [19]Then he took a loaf of bread, and when he had given thanks, he broke it and gave it to them, saying, "This is my body, which is given for you. Do this in remembrance of me." [20]And he did the same with the cup after supper, saying "This cup that is poured out for you is the new covenant in my blood. [21]But see, the one who betrays me is with me, and his hand is on the table. [22]For the Son of Man is going as it has been determined, but woe to that one by whom he is betrayed!" [23]Then they began to ask one another, which one of them it could be who would do this. [24]A dispute also arose among them as to which one of them was to be regarded as the greatest. [25]But he said to them, "The kings of the Gentiles lord it over them; and those in authority over them are called benefactors. [26]But not so with you; rather the greatest among you must become like the youngest, and the leader like one who serves. [27]For who is greater, the one who is at the table or the one who serves? Is it not the one at the table? But I am among you as one who serves. [28]You are those who have stood by me in my trials; [29]and I confer on you, just as my Father has conferred on me, a kingdom, [30]so that you may eat and drink at my table in my kingdom, and you will sit on thrones judging the twelve tribes of Israel. [31]Simon, Simon, listen! Satan has demanded to sift all of you like wheat, [32]but I have

prayed for you that your own faith may not fail; and you, when once you have turned back, strengthen your brothers.'' [33]And he said to him, ''Lord, I am ready to go with you to prison and to death!'' [34]Jesus said, ''I tell you, Peter, the cock will not crow this day, until you have denied three times that you know me.'' [35]He said to them, ''When I sent you out without a purse, bag, or sandals, did you lack anything?'' They said, ''No, not a thing.'' [36]He said to them, ''But now, the one who has a purse must take it, and likewise a bag. And the one who has no sword must sell his cloak and buy one. [37]For I tell you, this scripture must be fulfilled in me, 'And he was counted among the lawless'; and indeed what is written about me is being fulfilled.'' [38]They said, ''Lord, look, here are two swords.'' He replied, ''It is enough.'' [39]He came out and went, as was his custom, to the Mount of Olives; and the disciples followed him. [40]When he reached the place, he said to them, ''Pray that you may not come into the time of trial.'' [41]Then he withdrew from them about a stone's throw, knelt down, and prayed, [42]''Father, if you are willing, remove this cup from me; yet, not my will but yours be done.'' [43]Then an angel from heaven appeared to him and gave him strength. [44]In his anguish he prayed more earnestly, and his sweat became like great drops of blood falling down on the ground. [45]When he got up from prayer, he came to the disciples and found them sleeping because of grief, [46]and he said to them, ''Why are you sleeping? Get up and pray that you may not come into the time of trial.'' [47]While he was still speaking, suddenly a crowd came, and the one called Judas, one of the twelve, was leading them. He approached Jesus to kiss him; [48]but Jesus said to him, ''Judas, is it with a kiss that you are betraying the Son of Man?'' [49]When those who were around him saw what was coming, they asked, ''Lord, should we strike with the sword?'' [50]Then one of them struck the slave of the high priest and cut off his right ear. [51]But Jesus said, ''No more of this!'' And he touched his ear and healed him.

⁵²Then Jesus said to the chief priests, the officers of the temple police, and the elders who had come for him, "Have you come out with swords and clubs as if I were a bandit? ⁵³When I was with you day after day in the temple, you did not lay hands on me. But this is your hour, and the power of darkness!" ⁵⁴Then they seized him and led him away, bringing him into the high priest's house. But Peter was following at a distance. ⁵⁵When they had kindled a fire in the middle of the courtyard and sat down together, Peter sat among them. ⁵⁶Then a servant-girl, seeing him in the firelight, stared at him and said, "This man also was with him." ⁵⁷But he denied it, saying, "Woman, I do not know him." ⁵⁸A little later someone else, on seeing him, said, "You also are one of them." But Peter said, "Man, I am not!" ⁵⁹Then about an hour later still another kept insisting, "Surely this man also was with him; for he is a Galilean." ⁶⁰But Peter said, "Man, I do not know what you are talking about!" At that moment, while he was still speaking, the cock crowed. ⁶¹The Lord turned and looked at Peter. Then Peter remembered the word of the Lord, how he had said to him, "Before the cock crows today, you will deny me three times." ⁶²And he went out and wept bitterly. ⁶³Now the men who were holding Jesus began to mock him and beat him; ⁶⁴they also blindfolded him and kept asking him, "Prophesy! Who is it that struck you?" ⁶⁵They kept heaping many other insults on him. ⁶⁶When day came, the assembly of the elders of the people, both chief priests and scribes, gathered together, and they brought him to their council. ⁶⁷They said, "If you are the Messiah, tell us." He replied, "If I tell you, you will not believe; ⁶⁸and if I question you, you will not answer. ⁶⁹But from now on the Son of Man will be seated at the right hand of the power of God." ⁷⁰All of them asked, "Are you, then, the Son of God?" He said to them, "You say that I am." ⁷¹Then they said, "What further testimony do we need? We have heard it ourselves from his own lips!"

¹Then the assembly rose as a body and brought

Jesus before Pilate. [2]They began to accuse him, saying, "We found this man perverting our nation, forbidding us to pay taxes to the emperor, and saying that he himself is the Messiah, a king." [3]Then Pilate asked him, "Are you the king of the Jews?" He answered, "You say so." [4]Then Pilate said to the chief priests and the crowds, "I find no basis for an accusation against this man." [5]But they were insistent and said, "He stirs up the people by teaching throughout all Judea, from Galilee where he began even to this place." [6]When Pilate heard this, he asked whether the man was a Galilean. [7]And when he learned that he was under Herod's jurisdiction, he sent him off to Herod, who was himself in Jerusalem at that time. [8]When Herod saw Jesus, he was very glad, for he had been wanting to see him for a long time, because he had heard about him and was hoping to see him perform some sign. [9]He questioned him at some length, but Jesus gave him no answer. [10]The chief priests and the scribes stood by, vehemently accusing him. [11]Even Herod with his soldiers treated him with contempt and mocked him; then he put an elegant robe on him, and sent him back to Pilate. [12]That same day Herod and Pilate became friends with each other; before this they had been enemies. [13]Pilate then called together the chief priests, the leaders, and the people, [14]and said to them, "You brought me this man as one who was perverting the people; and here I have examined him in your presence and have not found this man guilty of any of your charges against him. [15]Neither has Herod, for he sent him back to us. Indeed, he has done nothing to deserve death. [16]I will therefore have him flogged and release him." [18]Then they all shouted out together, "Away with this fellow! Release Barabbas for us!" [19](This was a man who had been put in prison for an insurrection that had taken place in the city, and for murder.) [20]Pilate, wanting to release Jesus, addressed them again; [21]but they kept shouting "Crucify, crucify him!" [22]A third time he said to them, "Why, what evil has he done? I have found in him no ground for the sentence of death; I will therefore have him flogged and then release him.'' 23But they kept urgently demanding with loud shouts that he should be crucified; and their voices prevailed. 24So Pilate gave his verdict that their demand should be granted. 25He released the man they asked for, the one who had been put in prison for insurrection and murder, and he handed Jesus over as they wished. 26As they led him away, they seized a man, Simon of Cyrene, who was coming from the country, and they laid the cross on him, and made him carry it behind Jesus. 27A great number of the people followed him, and among them were women who were beating their breasts and wailing for him. 28But Jesus turned to them and said, ''Daughters of Jerusalem, do not weep for me, but weep for yourselves and for your children. 29For the days are surely coming when they will say, 'Blessed are the barren, and the wombs that never bore, and the breasts that never nursed.' 30Then they will begin to say to the mountains, 'Fall on us'; and to the hills, 'Cover us.' 31For if they do this when the wood is green, what will happen when it is dry?'' 32Two others also, who were criminals, were led away to be put to death with him. 33When they came to the place that is called The Skull, they crucified Jesus there with the criminals, one on his right and one on his left. 34Then Jesus said, ''Father, forgive them; for they do not know what they are doing.'' And they cast lots to divide his clothing. 35And the people stood by, watching; but the leaders scoffed at him, saying, ''He saved others; let him save himself if he is the Messiah of God, his chosen one!'' 36The soldiers also mocked him, coming up and offering him sour wine, 37and saying, ''If you are the King of the Jews, save yourself!'' 38There was also an inscription over him, ''This is the King of the Jews.'' 39One of the criminals who were hanged there kept deriding him and saying, ''Are you not the Messiah? Save yourself and us!'' 40But the other rebuked him, saying, ''Do you not fear God, since you are under the same sentence of condemnation? ⁴¹And we indeed have been condemned justly, for we are getting what we deserve for our deeds, but this man has done nothing wrong." ⁴²Then he said, "Jesus, remember me when you come into your kingdom." ⁴³He replied, "Truly I tell you, today you will be with me in Paradise." ⁴⁴It was now about noon, and darkness came over the whole land until three in the afternoon, ⁴⁵while the sun's light failed; and the curtain of the temple was torn in two. ⁴⁶Then Jesus, crying with a loud voice, said, "Father, into your hands I commend my spirit." Having said this, he breathed his last. When the centurion saw what had taken place, he praised God and said, "Certainly this man was innocent." ⁴⁸And when all the crowds who had gathered there for this spectacle saw what had taken place, they returned home, beating their breasts. ⁴⁹But all his acquaintances, including the women who had followed him from Galilee, stood at a distance, watching these things. ⁵⁰Now there was a good and righteous man named Joseph, who, though a member of the council, ⁵¹had not agreed to their plan and action. He came from the Jewish town of Arimathea, and he was waiting expectantly for the kindom of God. ⁵²This man went to Pilate and asked for the body of Jesus. ⁵³Then he took it down, wrapped it in a linen cloth, and laid it in a rock-hewn tomb where no one had ever been laid. ⁵⁴It was the day of Preparation, and the sabbath was beginning. ⁵⁵The women who had come with him from Galilee followed, and they saw the tomb and how his body was laid. ⁵⁶Then they returned, and prepared spices and ointments. On the sabbath they rested according to the commandment.

Luke 22:14 — 23:56

The betrayal, suffering, and death of Our Lord Jesus Christ.

We are present in the upper room. In these last hours Our Lord is handing on those symbols which will become the great centralities of Christian faith. Yet what do we see happening at the table? "A dispute also arose . . . as to which one of them was to be regarded as the greatest." If ever we feel that the New Testament shirks an honest portrait of the disciples this moment disproves us!

Next we overhear Jesus warn Simon that he is soon going to discover some dark things about himself. From there we enter the shadows of Gethsemane and see the pitiable inability of the disciples even to stay awake to support Jesus. Finally, they wake only to watch as Judas carries out his betrayal, shattering the trust of their whole group. They flee in every direction, terrified for their own survival. Peter alone follows only to find to his horror that he is vehemently denying any knowledge of this prisoner.

Then, in rapid succession, come the psychological and physical cruelty of the night's events. Blows are followed by jeers of "Who struck you?" Jesus stands before Pilate, this pitiable figure who embodies power but has no personal moral power. From there Jesus is dragged across the city to the decadent circle of Herod and his friends who cruelly mock the prisoner. Then we are back to the contemptible political squirming of Pilate, unable to justify a condemnation but nevertheless giving it. All the time we see the dark shadows gather in all human nature, including our own.

Two moments of light come into the darkness. Someone, albeit forced, shares the carrying of the cross. We do not in the least want to carry crosses but we too are forced to do so by life. An hour later there is the sublime gift of the dying thief. He makes it possible for the dying Jesus to discern in him a moment of response to the elusive kingdom which has cost so much. Beside him in the dark landscape stands Joseph of Arimathea, waiting to be faithful to the needs of Jesus' dead body, even if at some risk to himself.

Who are we in all this? We have encountered many facets of human nature. Most of it has been darkness shot through with a little light. Down deep we know we have seen our own portrait. There is much darkness in us. But there is also available to us the love and grace of him whom we have just seen suffering and dying. That is the Good News for this week.

Easter — during the Day

¹But on the first day of the week, at early dawn, they came to the tomb, taking the spices that they had prepared. ²They found the stone rolled away from the tomb, ³but when they went in, they did not find the body. ⁴While they were perplexed about this, suddenly two men in dazzling clothes stood beside them. ⁵The women were terrified and bowed their faces to the ground, but the men said to them, "Why do you look for the living among the dead? He is not here, but has risen. ⁶Remember how he told you, while he was still in Galilee, ⁷that the Son of Man must be handed over to sinners, and be crucified, and on the third day rise again." ⁸Then they remembered his words, ⁹and returning from the tomb, they told all this to the eleven and to all the rest.

Luke 24:1–9

As Our Lord rose from the tomb so also he seeks to rise in us.

It is so easy to be misled by the words "the first day of the week." All too easily we can imagine the women at the tomb of Jesus moving in the dawn of a quiet Sunday world. The reality is that they made their journey in a world waking up noisily to the beginning of another busy week. That morning for them was what Monday morning is for us! That can teach us something immediately: that it is precisely in the busy, bustling reality of our lives that you and I have to seek Our Lord.

"They came to the tomb." They came seeking the dead body of Jesus. So often we do that. We don't do it literally, but we do it thinking of Jesus as a long-ago figure, attractive, courageous, inspiring, but essentially separated from us by centuries, shut up in the tomb of history.

''They found the stone rolled away from the tomb.'' The stone which blocks our search for Our Lord is anything which prevents our seeing that Our Lord is not a dead memory but a living Lord. Sometimes it's the way in which we were taught about Our Lord. He may have been presented to us as a fascinating historical figure, but however fascinating he is not a risen, living reality. Not until our Christian faith has moved beyond being merely history or information or knowledge of the Bible do we discover Our Lord as our contemporary. With this discovery the stone has rolled away for us. We realize that Christian faith is not about someone lying in the tomb of the past; it is about one who is capable of being our friend.

''Why do you look for the living among the dead?'' We are all strongly tempted to seek what is living among things that are dead. Sometimes when we have had to leave a place we love we spend a long time searching for remembered experiences. Sometimes when we have been bereaved we lose the capacity to live in the present, and live in the past with that relationship. What we are looking for is love as a living thing, but all we can find in the past is the memory of a dead love.

''Returning from the tomb . . . to the eleven and to all the rest.'' The journey for every Christian must be from the deadness of mere information about Jesus to membership in the living body of Christian fellowship. That is the Good News for this week.

Second Sunday of Easter

[19]When it was evening on that day, the first day of the week, and the doors of the house where the disciples had met were locked for fear of the Jews, Jesus came and stood among them and said, "Peace be with you." [20]After he said this, he showed them his hands and his side. Then the disciples rejoiced when they saw the Lord. [21]Jesus said to them again, "Peace be with you. As the Father has sent me, so I send you." [22]When he had said this, he breathed on them and said to them, "Receive the Holy Spirit. [23]If you forgive the sins of any, they are forgiven them; if you retain the sins of any, they are retained." [24]But Thomas (who was called the twin), one of the twelve, was not with them when Jesus came. [25]So the other disciples told him, "We have seen the Lord." But he said to them, "Unless I see the mark of the nails in his hands, and put my finger in the mark of the nails and my hand in his side, I will not believe." [26]A week later his disciples were again in the house, and Thomas was with them. Although the doors were shut, Jesus came and stood among them and said, "Peace be with you." [27]Then he said to Thomas, "Put your finger here and see my hands. Reach out your hand and put it in my side. Do not doubt but believe." [28]Thomas answered him, "My Lord and my God!" [29]Jesus said to him, "Have you believed because you have seen me? Blessed are those who have not seen and yet have come to believe." [30]Now Jesus did many other signs in the presence of his disciples, which are not written in this book. [31]But these are written so that you may come to believe that Jesus is the Messiah, the Son of God, and that through believing you may have life in his name.

John 20:19–31

Doubt is universal and normal. It is not a betrayal of faith but often the anvil on which real faith is forged.

Many of us do not like to admit that our faith is permeated by many doubts. Faith and doubt are not confined to the affirmation or denial of facts and theories. Our personal experience can drag us into doubt that threatens the strongest faith. We may experience a tragedy in our lives so searing that our faith topples before it. We may not be able to see any meaning in the terrible thing that has happened or even in God. Doubt consumes faith and we feel helpless. In fact we may become so bitter we feel our faith was naive and unreal and deceived us.

This is the case with the disciple Thomas. Thomas in the Gospel appears to be a dour but stubbornly faithful man with few illusions about life. However, he is prepared to be faithful to this man Jesus, even to take risks with him.

At the time of this incident Thomas's worst fears have been realized. The disciples have all moved through the horror of Jesus' trial and execution and the shattering of their dreams. Now comes the unbelievable experience of their master's return. However, Thomas had left the group for a time. Coming back he is not only unbelieving but is also angry and rather contemptuous of their seeming delirium. Time passes and the risen Lord appears among them again. This time Thomas is there, and his acceptance is complete. For Thomas his master becomes ''My Lord and my God.''

Thomas's disbelief is not just that of a fundamentally doubting person. Thomas is a man who has given himself utterly to a person and to a dream: his commitment to Jesus is total. When you have given yourself like that and your trust is shattered you are almost incapable of believing again. You want to but you can't. When we love someone and that love is betrayed or taken from us we face a great struggle to love again. We don't want to risk giving it again. We have lost our trust in life.

In different ways many of us have experienced what Thomas experienced. Our Lord bids us live again and love again and trust again. He offers us resurrection. That is the Good News for this week.

Third Sunday of Easter

¹After these things Jesus showed himself again to the disciples by the Sea of Tiberias; and he showed himself in this way. ²Gathered there together were Simon Peter, Thomas called the Twin, Nathanael of Cana in Galilee, the sons of Zebedee, and two others of his disciples. ³Simon Peter said to them, "I am going fishing." They said to him, "We will go with you." They went out and got into the boat, but that night they caught nothing. ⁴Just after daybreak, Jesus stood on the beach; but the disciples did not know that it was Jesus. ⁵Jesus said to them, "Children, you have no fish, have you?" They answered him, "No." ⁶He said to them, "Cast the net to the right side of the boat, and you will find some." So they cast it, and now they were not able to haul it in because there were so many fish. ⁷That disciple whom Jesus loved said to Peter, "It is the Lord!" When Simon Peter heard that it was the Lord, he put on some clothes, for he was naked, and jumped into the sea. ⁸But the other disciples came in the boat, dragging the net full of fish, for they were not far from the land, only about a hundred yards off. ⁹When they had gone ashore, they saw a charcoal fire there, with fish on it, and bread. ¹⁰Jesus said to them, "Bring some of the fish that you have just caught." ¹¹So Simon Peter went aboard and hauled the net ashore, full of large fish, a hundred fifty-three of them; and though there were so many, the net was not torn. ¹²Jesus said to them, "Come and have breakfast." Now none of the disciples dared to ask him, "Who are you?" because they knew it was the Lord. ¹³Jesus came and took the bread and gave it to them, and did the same with the fish. ¹⁴This was now the third time that Jesus appeared to the disciples after he was raised from the dead. ¹⁵When they had finished breakfast, Jesus said to Simon Peter, "Simon son of John, do you

love me more than these?'' He said to him, ''Yes, Lord; you know that I love you.'' Jesus said to him, ''Feed my lambs.'' [16]A second time he said to him, ''Simon son of John, do you love me?'' He said to him, ''Yes, Lord; you know that I love you.'' Jesus said to him, ''Tend my sheep.'' [17]He said to him the third time, ''Simon, son of John, do you love me?'' Peter felt hurt because he said to him the third time, ''Do you love me?'' And he said to him, ''Lord, you know everything; you know that I love you.'' Jesus said to him, ''Feed my sheep. [18]Very truly, I tell you, when you were younger, you used to fasten your own belt and to go wherever you wished. But when you grow old, you will stretch out your hands, and someone else will fasten a belt around you and take you where you do not wish to go.'' [19](He said this to indicate the kind of death by which he would glorify God.) After this he said to him, ''Follow me.''

John 21:1–19

Our Lord shows us that failure can sometimes be the best preparation for accepting new responsibility.

''I am going fishing.'' When we experience bereavement or any other great shock we often take refuge in doing what is utterly familiar to us. We will insist on getting on with the housekeeping or going to the office. For the disciples Jesus is dead, their dreams are over, and there is nothing but to go back to what they have always done.

''You have no fish, have you?'' Could we imagine a more everyday thing to say at such a moment. There are no grandiloquent, stilted speeches; there is no obvious mystery. Here I am, he seems to say, real, approachable, alive, still very much involved in your lives, still your friend. We are seeing the beginning of the strong strain of the sacramental in Christian faith. Christ is Lord and King, but he is also present in the simplest ways, in such things as bread and wine.

"It is the Lord!" Notice the different reactions of the disciples, the different types among them. John is intuitive; he recognizes who it is. Peter's instinct is to swing into action. The others continue their task deliberately. As it takes all kinds to make this community, so it takes all kinds to make a study group or a committee or a congregation!

"Bring some of the fish." Notice how Our Lord makes sure that they bring something to this encounter. Their gifts and their work are important to his plans. Every time we bring our gifts to the altar we are doing the same thing. Our Lord is asking us for the blessings he has given us in the first place.

The conversation with Peter is fascinating. Peter and Jesus had unfinished business. In the upper room, on the night before the terror and the pain began, Jesus had told Peter he would fail. Peter had not accepted the possibility but it had happened, and he felt deeply ashamed. Here on the beach in the dawn we see Jesus putting this magnificent man back together again. Jesus is in effect telling Peter, and not only Peter but also every one of us, that it is all right to fail. Life doesn't end. In fact by calling Peter to a renewed vocation of leading the disciples into the future, Our Lord is pointing out that sometimes after we have failed we are better equipped for leadership. We are now more aware of our limitations, realistic about ourselves, and understanding of the weaknesses of others. That is the Good News for this week.

Fourth Sunday of Easter

²²At that time the festival of the Dedication took place in Jerusalem. It was winter, ²³and Jesus was walking in the temple, in the portico of Solomon. ²⁴So the Jews gathered around him and said to him, "How long will you keep us in suspense? If you are the Messiah, tell us plainly." ²⁵Jesus answered, "I have told you, and you do not believe. The works that I do in my Father's name testify to me; ²⁶but you do not believe, because you do not belong to my sheep. ²⁷My sheep hear my voice. I know them, and they follow me. ²⁸I give them eternal life, and they will never perish. No one will snatch them out of my hand. ²⁹What my Father has given me is greater than all else, and no one can snatch it out of the Father's hand. ³⁰The Father and I are one."

John 10:22–30

Getting and giving information about Jesus is important but by itself it cannot bring us to meet him as Lord. To do that we have to commit ourselves to a relationship with him.

"How long will you keep us in suspense? If you are the Messiah, tell us plainly." The question sounds genuine, asked by a Jew with an intense interest in who Jesus is and what he is doing. However Jesus' reply is almost sad, even frustrated, in tone. He says simply, "I have told you, and you do not believe," referring to countless occasions when he has tried to communicate and failed.

We look now how Jesus follows that initial weary expression of frustration. He points to things that he has done [v 25] as his evidence. He points also to the community he has formed around himself [v 27]. All of this is saying something to us in our own Christian experience.

First of all, back to that question Jesus is asked. Notice the words "tell us plainly." What was required was instruction, information, teaching. They wanted to be told in a straightforward way with no room for doubt. That was impossible. What Jesus was pointing to was a relationship between himself and God and between his followers and himself. That relationship grew when someone felt drawn to Jesus, and deepened as that person and Jesus spent time with each other, carried out tasks together. It was not a question of Jesus going to people, giving them some information or evidence which immediately persuaded them that they should follow him. Life is not like that, either then or now or ever. Relationships do not form because we are told anything about someone. They form by our being mutually drawn in a way that we sometimes can't even put into words.

That truth has consequences for Christians and for church life today. In personal life, reading and studying the life of Jesus as a figure in history is a worthwhile thing to do, but it is not sufficient to discover his reality. In congregational life, giving information, or "telling," or Christian education is very necessary but it is never enough. Life has to be lived together in community. Tasks have to be done, experiences shared. At the centre of all this is Our Lord and the Gospel about him. Living and doing and worshipping and experiencing together brings us into a relationship with him. Nobody can be just told that Jesus is Lord; each of us has to discover it. That is the Good News for this week.

Fifth Sunday of Easter

³¹When he had gone out, Jesus said, "Now the Son of Man has been glorified, and God has been glorified in him. ³²If God has been glorified in him, God will also glorify him in himself and will glorify him at once. ³³Little children, I am with you only a little longer. You will look for me; and as I said to the Jews so now I say to you, 'Where I am going you cannot come.' ³⁴I give you a new commandment, that you love another. Just as I have loved you, you also should love one another. ³⁵By this everyone will know that you are my disciples, if you have love for one another."

John 13:31–35

The shame and agony of Our Lord becomes something glorious for us because it reveals an unrealized divinity in our human nature.

We enter this passage at one of the most intense moments of our Lord's last hours. John allows us to eavesdrop in the shadows of the upper room as the last hours of Jesus' relationship with his disciples slip away. Just before, Judas, having received the piece of bread, has left to carry out his betrayal. As the door swings shut behind him we begin this passage.

"Now the Son of Man has been glorified." Like many of Our Lord's statements about the kingdom this one seems to fly in the face of any normal logic. How can imminent betrayal be called a glorifying of God? It must be that what is now to be achieved can be achieved only by this betrayal, suffering, and death.

"God has been glorified in him." We now try to view what is taking place from a point above time, trying to see this as the eye of God might see it. To our eyes this is an ordinary room; God sees it as the arena of the transformation and salvation of humanity! Something is going to happen within and beyond this room which is going to change the imprisonment of human nature. In this human being's response to all that is going to be inflicted upon him we are going to see human nature lifted to the ultimate level for which it was created. In a pathetic figure being sneered at, insulted, tried, beaten, lashed, and finally butchered on a cross, we are going to glimpse divinity in humanity. No wonder this betrayal is the beginning of a glorifying. Human nature is going to be shown the blinding glory of love and total self-giving which lies unrealized within it.

''Where I am going, you cannot come.'' Most certainly you and I cannot go this way. It is the way of ultimate love and ultimate self-sacrifice. However, because this Jesus has taken on the human nature which we share with him, he has by this ultimate self-sacrifice affected your nature and mine. Any self-giving we do, pitiable though it may be in comparison with this terrible sacrifice, will be because of the grace with which he has infected all human nature.

''I give you a new commandment.'' He is about to show us ultimate love in action, and all our attempts will be pale reflections of this love. Yet all he asks is that we love to the extent we can, for where we succeed, there he will always be. That is the Good News for this week.

Sixth Sunday of Easter

²³Jesus answered him, ''Those who love me will keep my word, and my Father will love them, and we will come to them and make our home with them. ²⁴Whoever does not love me does not keep my words; and the word that you hear is not mine, but is from the Father who sent me. ²⁵I have said these things to you while I am still with you. ²⁶But the Advocate, the Holy Spirit, whom the Father will send in my name, will teach you everything, and remind you of all that I have said to you. ²⁷Peace I leave with you; my peace I give to you. I do not give to you as the world gives. Do not let your hearts be troubled, and do not let them be afraid. ²⁸You heard me say to you, 'I am going away, and I am coming to you.' If you loved me, you would rejoice that I am going to the Father, because the Father is greater than I. ²⁹And now I have told you this before it occurs, so that when it does occur, you may believe.''

John 14:23–29

Our Lord is reflecting on our relationship with God, and we see how it resembles our human relationships.

Jesus has just been asked a question. Someone said to him, ''How is it that you will reveal yourself to us, and not to the world?'' The rest of this passage is Our Lord's reply. The first great truth is that Our Lord shows himself to the human heart. There are no vast planetary manifestations which some Christians have always longed for. Back in the desert Jesus was tempted to such displays and he rejected them. He came back to Galilee and captured human hearts one by one. In this upper room he is saying that it will always be this way. Evelyn Underhill in her poem "Immanence" expresses this perfectly, "I shall achieve My Immemorial Plan. / Pass the low lintel of the human heart."

"Those who love me will keep my Word." Our Lord shows us love in terms of obedient action. Love is not just a feeling or a sentiment. Where there is love there is obedience. Where obedience does not exist neither does love.

"We will come to them and make our home with them." If we live a life of intentional obedience to God as we have experienced that God in Our Lord, then a relationship is formed. It goes without saying that this relationship will never be constant or perfect. Our human nature will interfere and put up blocks; faith will go through periods of confidence and periods of doubt. But if we strive for an obedient life we will have moments of natural encounter with the Lord who is both the source of our obedience and its object.

"The Advocate, the Holy Spirit . . . will teach you everything." Our relationship with Our Lord, like our human relationships, must grow and deepen if it is to be real. My childhood relationship with God, while it affects all my subsequent life, will not suffice for my adult life. The tragedy is that this truth is so often not realized.

"I am going away, and I am coming to you." It is a deliberate paradox whose truth is borne out again and again in our human relationships. This is true between parents and children. If it does not happen the relationship cannot develop. The same is true in our relationship with God. Each stage of it must change, i.e., "go away," so that the next stage can develop, i.e., "come again." That is the Good News for this week.

Ascension of the Lord

⁴⁶And he said to them, "Thus it is written, that the Messiah is to suffer and to rise from the dead on the third day, ⁴⁷and that repentance and forgiveness of sins is to be proclaimed in his name to all nations, beginning from Jerusalem. ⁴⁸You are witnesses of these things. ⁴⁹And see, I am sending upon you what my Father promised; so stay here in the city until you have been clothed with power from on high." ⁵⁰Then he led them out as far as Bethany, and lifting up his hands, he blessed them. ⁵¹While he was blessing them, he withdrew from them and was carried up into heaven. ⁵²And they worshiped him, and returned to Jerusalem with great joy; ⁵³and they were continually in the temple blessing God.

Luke 24:46–53

When Jesus left his disciples he did so only to return into every one of their lives. He can return to our lives as well.

This passage which brings Saint Luke's Gospel to an end is not actually an ending, it's really a beginning. Although it marks the end of Our Lord's being among the disciples in a visible, objective way, it also shows them being called to the beginning of a new responsibility. They had seen Jesus die, and had scattered, demoralised and defeated. Then the unbelievable had happened: he came among them again. Although he was changed, the disciples were quite sure it was the Lord whom they had known and followed for the last few years. From time to time he reappeared: to all of them in Jerusalem, to Mary in the garden, to a group fishing in Galilee, to a couple on the road to Emmaus.

It is just after this last encounter that this Gospel

passage begins. The two disciples have just come running back from Emmaus. They have gasped out the story of their encounter with what they had thought was a stranger. In the simple action of his breaking a piece of bread they realized that the person with them was far from being a stranger. It was their Lord!

The news electrifies the rest of the disciples into all sorts of thoughts and hopes and plans. Suddenly, Jesus is among them. Once again, he explains the meaning of all that has happened and is happening. He reassures them that the world is not falling apart. The ghastly cross was part of a great plan, and his coming from the tomb was the climax and triumph of that plan. Now something new must begin in and through them. What has happened has to be communicated, and that task is in their hands.

This Gospel's point is that *we* are those whom Jesus calls disciples. Whatever was said in that long-ago encounter after the resurrection is being said again to-day and will be said in every age. Ours are the ears that hear him — or choose not to hear him — today.

Jesus was asking for his disciples' commitment, and he asks the same of us. If we commit ourselves to him he promises us what he promised those men and women. He promises his Spirit, the Spirit we call the Holy Spirit, in our deepest being. It's a real promise which millions of men and women have found to be true. If we say Yes to him giving him our spirit, poor and limited though it may be, he gives us his. We get much the better side of the bargain!

Our Lord ended this last encounter by gathering the disciples, blessing them, and going from them. As people have discovered in every generation since, he went away only to return into every one of their lives. He has already returned to yours and mine; all we need to do is to realize it. That is the Good News for this week.

Seventh Sunday of Easter

²⁰"I ask not only on behalf of these, but also on behalf of those who will believe in me through their word, ²¹that they may all be one. As you, Father, are in me and I am in you, may they also be in us, so that the world may believe that you have sent me. ²²The glory that you have given me I have given them, so that they may be one, as we are one, ²³I in them and you in me, that they may become completely one, so that the world may know that you have sent me and have loved them even as you have loved me. ²⁴Father, I desire that those also, whom you have given me, may be with me where I am, to see my glory, which you have given me because you loved me before the foundation of the world. ²⁵Righteous Father, the world does not know you, but I know you; and these know that you have sent me. ²⁶I made your name known to them, and I will make it known, so that the love with which you have loved me may be in them, and I in them."

John 17:20–26

In his last hours with his disciples Our Lord prays passionately for their unity. He is also praying for the same unity for all Christians.

As we read the Gospel according to John we can find ourselves in very deep waters. More than any other Gospel writer, John recalls the reflections of Our Lord. Most of these long reflections are from the last hours Jesus spent with his disciples. There are many levels of meaning and we have to probe very deeply for them.

As we begin this passage we are listening to Jesus as

he nears the end of his great prayer for the disciples. Our Lord knows that there is very little time left before he is taken. Here around this table are the hands which will be his hands, the tongues which will speak for him. He knows all too well their humanity and their limitations. All this we hear in the intensity of every thought in his prayer. Above all he prays that this group will remain united amid all that the future brings.

''I ask . . . [for] those who will believe in me through their word.'' Jesus is now praying for the church that will form from the lives of these men. When we think about that for a moment we realize that Jesus is reaching out across the centuries and praying for us!

''That they may be one, as we are one.'' All through this prayer Jesus is asking that the relationship among his disciples may resemble the relationship that he himself has with the Father. Everything that we know of that relationship shows that it was one of the deepest intimacy. So we know that Our Lord wishes this intimacy and trust to exist within the life of the church. How very much we have to struggle for that in contemporary church life, at least in our North American culture. Congregations, especially large congregations, find both unity and intimacy elusive. Unity is difficult because of the wide spectrum of opinions and attitudes in today's society. Some congregations find that the development of small groups can achieve intimacy for some people. The exchanging of the peace, though it may be difficult for some individuals and seems intrusive for others, is an attempt to remind us that in Jesus Chrsit we are called to be one. If we have any doubt at all about that we have only to read this prayer in its entirety! That is the Good News for this week.

The Day of Pentecost

[8]Philip said to him, "Lord, show us the Father, and we will be satisfied." [9]Jesus said to him, "Have I been with you all this time, Philip, and you still do not know me? Whoever has seen me has seen the Father. How can you say, 'Show us the Father'? [10]Do you not believe that I am in the Father and the Father is in me? The words that I say to you I do not speak on my own; but the Father who dwells in me does his works. [11]Believe me that I am in the Father and the Father is in me; but if you do not, then believe me because of the works themselves. [12]Very truly, I tell you, the one who believes in me will also do the works that I do and, in fact, will do greater works than these; because I am going to the Father. [13]I will do whatever you ask in my name, so that the Father may be glorified in the Son. [14]If in my name you ask me for anything, I will do it. [15]If you love me, you will keep my commandments. [16]And I will ask the Father, and he will give you another Advocate, to be with you forever. [17]This is the Spirit of truth, whom the world cannot receive, because it neither sees him nor knows him. You know him, because he abides with you, and he will be in you. [25]I have said these things to you while I am still with you. [26]But the Advocate, the Holy Spirit, whom the Father will send in my name, will teach you everything, and remind you of all that I have said to you. [27]Peace I leave with you; my peace I give to you. I do not give to you as the world gives. Do not let your hearts be troubled, and do not let them be afraid."

John 14:8–17, 25–27

Our Lord speaks to his disciples and to us of his life being both our window to God and our introduction to the Holy Spirit.

All through these weeks after Easter millions of Christians are reading this Gospel according to John. We are going back over all the things Jesus said to his disciples in the upper room before he was crucified. Why? Because now we know he is risen, we can hear them in a new way.

"Philip said to him, Lord, show us the Father." Philip wants certainty and all of us want that from time to time, especially when our faith is being strained and we are no longer sure of anything. We long for that specific response from God that leaves no doubt.

"Whoever has seen me has seen the Father." It is very important that Jesus does not say he "is" the Father; he says that he "is in" the Father. No further nagging is going to get us very far because at this moment we are at the very heart of the great Christian mystery, the mystery we call the Incarnation, the interfacing in Jesus Christ of humanity and divinity. We can ask our "how" questions for ever and we cannot unravel this mystery.

"The one who believes in me will also do the works that I do." All we know is that in some way when we look at Jesus we are looking through a window toward God. What Our Lord says to us is what God wants to say to us. Our Lord's actions are his carrying out of the will of God in the world: if our actions in any way reflect those of Our Lord then we are carrying out the will and nature of God.

"If you love me, you will keep my commandments." Once again we hear Jesus link love to obedience. Love for Our Lord is never just a nice feeling. Love abides where there is obedience to him.

"He [the Father] will give you another Advocate." Here is a frequent theme of Our Lord. He was saying that his disciples' relationship with him could not stop at this point, it was only beginning. In fact, the relationship would have to grow all their lives. Jesus says the same to each of us. The relationship between a Christian and his or her Lord must be constantly growing. That is the Good News for this week.

Trinity Sunday

12"I still have many things to say to you, but you cannot bear them now. 13When the Spirit of truth comes, he will guide you into all the truth; for he will not speak on his own, but will speak whatever he hears, and he will declare to you the things that are to come. 14He will glorify me, because he will take what is mine and declare it to you. 15All that the Father has is mine. For this reason I said that he will take what is mine and declare it to you.

John 16:12–15

Our pilgrimage in Christ is never done. We are always being called to further insight and inspiration.

We are still in these wonderful hours of reflection which Jesus shared in the upper room. Jesus saw the shadowed walls of that room fade away, and looked across time and generations to all those who would come to these words and find grace in them.

"I still have many things to say to you but you cannot bear them now." What incalculable challenges are here! Our Lord is telling us that Christian experience has no horizon. Even to say this fills one with awe. Is Our Lord not promising to call Christians to further discovery until the end of time, and give us grace to live in our world of turmoil and ambiguity. If Our Lord is pushing at the frontiers of Christian thinking in his earthly time, he is doing so again in our present time of massive change.

"When the spirit of truth comes, he will guide you into all the truth." Again we have this assurance that the adventure is always just beginning. It was just beginning for the listening disciples that long-ago night, yet there is a sense in which it is only beginning for us two thousand years later. If God be truly God then there is no end to what can be discovered, learned, and lived. This thought rings through the verse of ''Amazing Grace'' which says ''When we've been there ten thousand years, bright shining as the sun; we've no less days to sing God's praise than when we first begun.''

''All that the Father has is mine.'' Perhaps we could use this statement of Jesus to point out something about the world of spirituality of our time. In the sixties many felt that other great world spiritualities had insights and disciplines that Christian tradition lacked. What we are finding more and more is that if only we search the Christian tradition it provides all that we can ask for. In one of his letters Paul wishes Christians to realize that in Christ they possess all things. Here Our Lord himself promises us to have all we need in our search for God. That is the Good News for this week.

Sunday between 5 and 11 June

¹¹Soon afterwards he went to a town called Nain, and his disciples and a large crowd went with him. ¹²As he approached the gate of the town, a man who had died was being carried out. He was his mother's only son, and she was a widow; and with her was a large crowd from the town. ¹³When the Lord saw her, he had compassion for her and said to her, "Do not weep." ¹⁴Then he came forward and touched the bier, and the bearers stood still. And he said, "Young man, I say to you, rise!" ¹⁵The dead man sat up and began to speak, and Jesus gave him to his mother. ¹⁶Fear seized all of them; and they glorified God, saying, "A great prophet has risen among us!" and "God has looked favorably on his people!" ¹⁷This word about him spread throughout Judea and all the surrounding country.

Luke 7:11–17

There are times in our lives when we feel dead, when Our Lord bids us to come alive again and gives us grace to do so.

As we encounter Jesus and his work in the Gospel, we are constantly faced with two things. The first is that Jesus saw his vocation very largely in terms of healing. He spent a great deal of time healing people of every description and of every kind of disease. We always want to know how Jesus did these things. There is no harm in this question as long as we realize that it will never be fully answered. In Jesus of Nazareth we encounter a person with an extraordinary gift of healing. Our Lord has shared this gift with many men and women in every age. These people, far from being mysterious or exotic, have often been excrutiatingly ordinary.

What they have in common is a complete absence of any illusion that they themselves are the source of healing. They know themselves to be mere channels of their healing Lord.

"The dead man sat up." With Our Lord we must go further. There are occasions in the Gospel, such as this one, which are told with the immediacy and simplicity of absolute, factual truth. Here, we can say one of two things, each of which gives glory to Our Lord. We can conclude that the young man was actually dead and that there stood beside him the one actual conquerer of death who has ever walked this earth. On the other hand, we could believe that among Jesus' healing powers was the capacity to tell death from coma. William Temple, one of the great and devout Christian minds of this century, remarked of the healing of Jairus's daughter that he could never understand how we presume it to be a raising of the dead when Jesus categorically said that the child was not dead but asleep.

There is a further way in which a passage such as this can speak to our lives. What does it mean to say you and I are "carried out of the city dead"? It means those many occasions when we head home in the evening, parts of us in a sense dead, numbed by a hurt done to us, a cutting remark, a threat made, a mistake we couldn't avoid, a harsh confrontation, some hours of tension. Sometimes we can use the privacy of the journey home to allow Jesus to touch us by his loving compassion. We can hear him bid us to come alive again. That is the Good News for this week.

Sunday between 12 and 18 June

[36]One of the Pharisees asked Jesus to eat with him, and he went into the Pharisee's house and took his place at the table. [37]And a woman in the city, who was a sinner, having learned that he was eating in the Pharisee's house, brought an alabastar jar of ointment. [38]She stood behind him at his feet, weeping, and began to bathe his feet with her tears and to dry them with her hair. Then she continued kissing his feet and anointing them with the ointment. [39]Now when the Pharisee who had invited him saw it, he said to himself, "If this man were a prophet, he would have known who and what kind of woman this is who is touching him — that she is a sinner." [40]Jesus spoke up and said to him, "Simon, I have something to say to you." "Teacher," he replied, "Speak." [41]"A certain creditor had two debtors: one owed five hundred denarii, and the other fifty. [42]When they could not pay, he canceled the debts for both of them. Now which of them will love him more?" [43]Simon answered, "I suppose the one for whom he canceled the greater debt." And Jesus said to him, "You have judged rightly." [44]Then turning toward the woman, he said to Simon, "Do you see this woman? I entered your house; you gave me no water for my feet, but she has bathed my feet with her tears and dried them with her hair. [45]You gave me no kiss, but from the time I came in she has not stopped kissing my feet. [46]You did not anoint my head with oil, but she has anointed my feet with ointment. [47]Therefore, I tell you, her sins, which were many, have been forgiven; hence she has shown great love. But the one to whom little is forgiven, loves little." [48]Then he said to her, "Your sins are forgiven." [49]But those who were at the table with him began to say among themselves, "Who is this who even forgives sins?" [50]And he said to the

woman, "Your faith has saved you; go in peace."

¹Soon afterwards he went on through cities and villages, proclaiming and bringing the good news of the kingdom of God. The twelve were with him, ²as well as some women who had been cured of evil spirits and infirmities: Mary, called Magdalene, from whom seven demons had gone out, ³and Joanna, the wife of Herod's steward Chuza, and Susanna, and many others, who provided for them out of their resources.

Luke 7:36—8:3

To have no illusions about ourselves, to realize who and what we are, and at the same time to know that God accepts us, is to taste the kingdom of God.

A theme constantly in Jesus' teaching and very near to his heart was the necessity for forgiveness in human relationships. The day his disciples asked him to teach them to pray Our Lord put the issue of forgiveness at the heart of our relationship with God. In two simple and inseparable petitions he teaches us for all time that forgiveness is conditional. We cannot be forgiven unless we ourselves are forgiving people.

I mention this because something very like it is at the heart of this episode. It was customary at a meal in the Graeco-Roman style for strangers to stand around the edge of the room in the shadows. They might be poor or in some other need. They might be trying to attract the attention of a prominent guest from whom they wished a favour. In Jesus' case a woman wants to thank him. She does so very effusively and passionately. Jesus' host is silently appalled by her behaviour and Our Lord notices.

How does Our Lord deal with the situation? From what he says we can assume that he and the woman have had a previous encounter. She is known as a sinner, possibly a prostitute. It is obvious that Jesus has made all the difference in her life, probably making it possible for her to deal with the anger and self-hatred which are part of her existence. Anger and self-hatred are part of many of our lives and to get his point across Jesus tells a story. Its message is that the greater a person's sense of being forgiven the greater the gratitude will be. Jesus then applies this to our inner lives. The key statement Jesus makes is in verse 47. "I tell you, her sins, which were many, have been forgiven; hence she has shown great love. But the one to whom little is forgiven, loves little."

This theme obviously was central in Jesus' thinking. We hear it in the parable of the pharisee and the publican in the temple. We hear it again in the story of the prodigal son. On each occasion Our Lord seems to be saying that to realize without illusion who we are, to realize how little we can claim to be, yet at that same moment to realize that we are accepted by God precisely on these terms, is to discover the secret of inner freedom and inner acceptance. To taste this is to taste the kingdom of God. That is the Good News for this week.

Sunday between 19 and 25 June

18Once when Jesus was praying alone, with only the disciples near him, he asked them, ''Who do the crowds say that I am?'' 19They answered, ''John the Baptist; but others, Elijah; and still others, that one of the ancient prophets has arisen.'' 20He said to them, ''But who do you say that I am?'' Peter answered, ''The Messiah of God.'' 21He sternly ordered and commanded them not to tell anyone, 22saying, ''The Son of Man must undergo great suffering, and be rejected by the elders, chief priests, and scribes, and be killed, and on the third day be raised.'' 23Then he said to them all, ''If any want to become my followers, let them deny themselves and take up their cross daily and follow me. 24For those who want to save their life will lose it, and those who lose their life for my sake will save it.''

Luke 9:18–24

Jesus asks us the question he asked his disciples. It forces us to decide who he is for us.

''Once when Jesus was praying alone.'' Very few of us in our western culture find it easy to set aside time for prayer. Most of us are always ''going to.'' Some of us are busy reading the latest little book on prayer with its good ideas about setting time aside, but even though the shelves are groaning with helpful books we still find it difficult. Jesus constantly set aside time for prayer, and that statement should speak to us deeply. If he needed to how much more do we!

''Jesus was praying alone, with only the disciples near him.'' This sounds like a contradiction, but it may be saying something to us. If we wait for perfect moments to try to be alone with Our Lord we are going to wait a long time. Modern life provides very few, if any, islands of perfect peace. We need to cultivate the art of being alone among other people, among other duties, deadlines, responsibilities.

"He said to them . . . 'who do you say that I am?'" He is asking each one of us, Who is Jesus Christ for me? Is he a childhood memory, an inspiration in a certain time of my idealistic youth, an interesting historic figure? Or, is he more than that? Do I think of him as contemporary in my life? Do I consciously seek his presence at any time in my demanding schedule? Does his life set standards for mine? Do I have at least a working knowledge of what the Gospel writers tell me about his life? All of these questions and many more are contained in Jesus' deceptively simple question to his disciples.

"Peter answered, 'The Messiah of God.'" Is that our answer? If it is, what is the response in our lives? If the word Messiah means an anointed one, a king and ruler, then we are asking ourselves to what extent Christ is authoritative in our lives. To what extent do we give him significance and authority when we are making decisions?

"If any want to become my followers." Jesus says two things are necessary. First, we must take responsibility for our lives, i.e., "take up [our] cross." We must come to terms with our own self-centredness, i.e., "deny [our]selves." We cannot do that just in bursts of religious enthusiasm; we have to do it "daily." Secondly, we have to discover the great truth that the more we give, or lose ourselves, in life, the more we get or find or save. That is the Good News for this week.

Sunday between 26 June and 2 July

^{51}When the days drew near for him to be taken up, he set his face to go to Jerusalem. ^{52}And he sent messengers ahead of him. On their way they entered a village of the Samaritans to make ready for him; ^{53}but they did not receive him, because his face was set toward Jerusalem. ^{54}When his disciples James and John saw it, they said, ''Lord, do you want us to command fire to come down from heaven and consume them?'' ^{55}But he turned and rebuked them. ^{56}Then they went on to another village. ^{57}As they were going along the road, someone said to him, ''I will follow you wherever you go.'' ^{58}And Jesus said to him, ''Foxes have holes, and birds of the air have nests; but the Son of Man has nowhere to lay his head.'' ^{59}To another he said, ''Follow me.'' But he said, ''Lord, first let me go and bury my father.'' ^{60}But Jesus said to him ''Let the dead bury their own dead; but as for you, go and proclaim the kingdom of God.'' ^{61}Another said, ''I will follow you, Lord; but let me first say farewell to those at my home.'' ^{62}Jesus said to him, ''No one who puts a hand to the plow and looks back is fit for the kingdom of God.''

Luke 9:51–62

Our Lord warns us that we can become so locked into our patterns of life that we can never break free and grow.

''He set his face to go to Jerusalem.'' Anyone who thinks of Jesus as being dragged unwillingly to his fate has only to look at this statement. His decisions are made with complete awareness of the possible consequences. Jesus is never the helpless victim of events, the well-meaning but unlucky character in the drama. He is in charge, not in any domineering sense but in the sense that he is a totally free person, who knows the human situation and the cost. Now he sets out. That is not a bad way to live our own lives.

"Entered a village of the Samaritans." Jews did not go through Samaria. While it was not regarded exactly as enemy country, it was an area to be despised and avoided. However, Jesus was not prepared to write off a whole community in that facile way. We might take a moment to ask where our "Samaria" is, those areas of our lives, whether they be communities or races or individuals, which down deep we despise for reasons we could not really justify if challenged.

We now see Jesus in two very different situations; his reactions are interesting. The first situation is one of rejection. The Samaritan village is not ready to accept the group. The disciples are enraged. Here they are being generously "liberal" to these people and they don't appreciate it! How dare they! Notice how the latent hatred and violence flash out in James and John. But Jesus "rebuked them."

The second incident is one of seeming acceptance. Someone comes to Jesus and offers to follow him "wherever you go." We all feel wary of expansive gestures made in an enthusiastic mood. They have obviously not been thought through and the person's chances of following through are slim. Jesus issues a warning about the cost of this emotional offer and the person seems to fade away.

Next Jesus invites a person to follow him. As you and I read this passage the invitation comes to us. The man asks for time to bury his father. Jesus says what in that culture was a shocking thing: "Let the dead bury their own dead." As with many of his statements, Our Lord was resorting to extreme language to make a point. Yet, we can let the past so capture us that we can never get free of it, so we never change and grow. However, with Our Lord's grace we can. That is the Good News for this week.

Sunday between 3 and 9 July

¹After this the Lord appointed seventy others and sent them on ahead of him in pairs to every town and place where he himself intended to go. ²He said to them, "The harvest is plentiful, but the laborers are few; therefore ask the Lord of the harvest to send out laborers into his harvest. ³Go on your way. See, I am sending you out like lambs into the midst of wolves. ⁴Carry no purse, no bag, no sandals; and greet no one on the road. ⁵Whatever house you enter, first say, 'Peace in this house!' ⁶And if anyone is there who shares in peace, your peace will rest on that person; but if not, it will return to you. ⁷Remain in the same house, eating and drinking whatever they provide, for the laborer deserves to be paid. Do not move about from house to house. ⁸Whenever you enter a town and its people welcome you, eat what is set before you; ⁹cure the sick who are there, and say to them, 'The kingdom of God has come near to you.' ¹⁰But whenever you enter a town and they do not welcome you, go out into its streets and say, ¹¹'Even the dust of your town that clings to our feet, we wipe off in protest against you. Yet know this: the kingdom of God has come near.' ¹²I tell you, on that day it will be more tolerable for Sodom than for that town. ¹⁷The seventy returned with joy, saying, "Lord, in your name even the demons submit to us!" ¹⁸He said to them, "I watched Satan fall from heaven like a flash of lightning. ¹⁹See, I have given you authority to tread on snakes and scorpions, and over all the power of the enemy; and nothing will hurt you. ²⁰Nevertheless, do not rejoice at this, that the spirits submit to you, but rejoice that your names are written in heaven."

Luke 10:1–12, 17–20

As we watch Jesus send people out on an essentially healing mission, we realize that healing may be Christians' primary vocation in a world of great dis-ease.

Our Lord began by drawing around him a small circle of

twelve disciples; it was the number of Israel's tribes. Because he felt that his task was to form a new people of God, a new Israel, he took this number as symbolic.

Our Lord now takes the next step in his mission to the world. He selects seventy people and sends them into the surrounding countryside two by two. One thing we can't help noticing is that there are very few directions. They are "to greet no one on the road." They are to say "Peace to this house." They are to accept hospitality. If they are not received they are to leave. In addition, they are told to heal the sick, and say to them "The kingdom of God has come near to you."

As with any passage of scripture there is something for us as we try to be Christian in today's world. By telling them not to greet anyone on the road — eastern salutations were lengthy and elaborate — Jesus was giving their task a sense of urgency. We need that sense in some tasks we take on as Christians. Very often in church life we can lack a sense of urgency about what we are doing: we regard our church commitments as casual and of rather law priority.

It should be very significant for Christian life today that the only specific action Jesus commands is to heal the sick. Increasingly for contemporary Christians the healing ministry is strong and widespread. Furthermore, there is a realization that in a frantic and tense and fearful world the great power of Christian faith can be to bring healing to the lives of individuals — the healing of fears, angers, anxieties. Perhaps just as valuable is the ability of Christian faith to bring a renewed sense of meaning and purpose into people's lives. Another vast area in which Christian faith is immensely healing is where its truths are expressed in the insights of psychology. Many people have good reason to know that when both of these gifts of God are used together they can be deeply healing. Our generation of Christians may well be called to a ministry whose primary task is healing, both in individual lives as well as in social and political situations. That is the Good News for this week.

Sunday between 10 and 16 July

²⁵Just then a lawyer stood up to test Jesus. "Teacher," he said, "what must I do to inherit eternal life?" ²⁶He said to him, "What is written in the law? What do you read there?" ²⁷He answered, "You shall love the Lord your God with all your heart, and with all your soul, and with all your strength, and with all your mind; and your neighbor as yourself." ²⁸And he said to him, "You have given the right answer; do this, and you will live." ²⁹But wanting to justify himself, he asked Jesus, "And who is my neighbor?" ³⁰Jesus replied, "A man was going down from Jerusalem to Jericho, and fell into the hands of robbers, who stripped him, beat him, and went away, leaving him half dead. ³¹Now by chance a priest was going down that road; and when he saw him, he passed by on the other side. ³²So likewise a Levite, when he came to the place and saw him, passed by on the other side. ³³But a Samaritan while traveling came near him; and when he saw him, he was moved with pity. ³⁴He went to him and bandaged his wounds, having poured oil and wine on them. Then he put him on his own animal, brought him to an inn, and took care of him. ³⁵The next day he took out two denarii, gave them to the innkeeper, and said, 'Take care of him; and when I come back, I will repay you whatever more you spend.' ³⁶Which of these three, do you think, was a neighbor to the man who fell into the hands of the robbers?" ³⁷He said, "The one who showed him mercy." Jesus said to him, "Go and do likewise."

Luke 10:25–37

Our Lord suggests that we can be surprised if we form stereotypes. The term *Samaritan* has many equivalents today.

Luke tells us that the lawyer asked his question to test Jesus, and it may have been insincere. But the question is one we all ask. Instead, we may say, What is worth giving your life to? but we are asking the same question.

Jesus replied, "What is written in the law?" Jesus doesn't push; he intuits our level, then lets us decide how deeply we want to go. The lawyer wants to go further. Jesus realizes that although this man has hidden agenda, and may even have treacherous motives, the questions are genuine if only because they are universal.

The second question, Who is my neighbour? is one of the great questions of our own age. In a world of lonely condominiums, security-surrounded housing estates, teeming airports, who is my neighbour? In a world where my very welcome stock dividends may involve the exploitation of someone ten thousand miles away, someone who may actually share the eucharistic chalice in my own tradition on the other side of the world, who is my neighbour?

The story with which Jesus responds is many levelled in meaning. The one who provides help is a Samaritan. This was culturally shocking to that Jewish audience. It was like showing up the behaviour of two prominent white citizens of a southern city in the United States in the 1960s by contrasting it with that of a compassionate black! How does the story challenge our own realized and unrealized stereotypes?

Notice how the levels of care assumed by the Samaritan challenge our capacity to care. First he binds up the man's wounds. Then, he could have left feeling that he had done what was reasonably required of him. But he takes the man to an inn and pays for his keep. Finally, he tells of his intention to return to continue his concern. He is prepared to involve a great deal of himself in this man. In our society, by and large, that kind of caring is hard to come by. We find that the special gesture is quite possible. The generous cheque, the one-time visit, are possible, but we tend to be wary of any longer commitment. We look for the organization that can take over. Our Lord calls us not only to care until cure is achieved, but also to continue to care even when cure is not possible. That is the Good News for this week.

Sunday between 17 and 23 July

[38]Now as they went on their way, he entered a certain village, where a woman named Martha welcomed him into her home. [39]She had a sister named Mary, who sat at the Lord's feet and listened to what he was saying. [40]But Martha was distracted by her many tasks; so she came to him and asked, ''Lord, do you not care that my sister has left me to do all the work by myself? Tell her then to help me.'' [41]But the Lord answered her, ''Martha, Martha, you are worried and distracted by many things; [42]there is need of only one thing. Mary has chosen the better part, which will not be taken away from her.''

Luke 10:38–42

We have a constant struggle between being and doing. Our Lord names this struggle in two of his friends.

In a few vivid words Luke draws the picture of these two sisters. They are opposites in temperament. Martha receives Jesus into the house, and one gets the impression that this is typically Martha, continually driven to take on new tasks even if she is already borne down with duties. It also indicates an instinctive generosity and hospitality. Martha is an extrovert. Then, in a single image, Mary is presented to us as an introvert. She sits listening, passive in contrast to Martha's incessant activity.

What is significant is that Martha is not merely busy, she is ''distracted,'' Luke tells us. There is a difference. There are people who can be intensely active and busy with cool efficiency. Such people can pace themselves; they have a high level of energy but all is organized. Not so Martha.

She is a driven personality with far too many commitments and deadlines. Martha does it to herself!

We notice something else about Martha. Because she resents what she is doing to herself, she has developed an angry resentment towards her sister [v 40]. It is obvious that she doesn't want to deal with this resentment because she tries to get Jesus to admonish her sister!

Martha's busyness is neurotic, and Jesus sees this very clearly. It springs from inner agenda she is not dealing with. He uses the terms "worried and distracted." Our culture breeds this kind of personality. Many of us know Martha's helplessness in our own anxious drive. As with Martha, Our Lord tries to get us to bring into our lives "one thing" which he calls "the better part." It's a part of ourselves that for some reason we don't cultivate. We can't quieten our mind, and, fearing the prospect of trying, we keep our bodies active with endless self-created responsibilities. If we are this kind of person we find that people who can be still actually annoy us, as Mary annoys Martha! Jesus is not saying that Mary is right to allow Martha to do everything, he is merely pointing out to Martha that she needs to cultivate some of her sister's inner stillness.

Mary and Martha work out their uneasy relationship not only in that long-ago house in Bethany but also in most of our own daily lives. What this passage illustrates is the constant effort to balance being and doing in our lives. That is the Good News for this week.

Sunday between 24 and 30 July

¹He was praying in a certain place, and after he had finished, one of his disciples said to him, "Lord, teach us to pray, as John taught his disciples." ²He said to them, "When you pray, say: Father, hallowed be your name. Your kingdom come. ³Give us each day our daily bread. ⁴And forgive us our sins, for we ourselves forgive everyone indebted to us. And do not bring us to the time of trial." ⁵And he said to them, "Suppose one of you has a friend, and you go to him at midnight and say to him, 'Friend, lend me three loaves of bread; ⁶for a friend of mine has arrived, and I have nothing to set before him.' ⁷And he answers from within, 'Do not bother me; the door has already been locked, and my children are with me in bed; I cannot get up and give you anything.' ⁸I tell you, even though he will not get up and give him anything because he is his friend, at least because of his persistence he will get up and give him whatever he needs. ⁹So I say to you, Ask, and it will be given you; search, and you will find; knock, and the door will be opened for you. ¹⁰For everyone who asks receives, and everyone who searches finds, and for everyone who knocks, the door will be opened. ¹¹Is there anyone among you who, if your child asks for a fish, will give a snake instead of a fish? ¹²Or if the child asks for an egg, will give a scorpion? ¹³If you then, who are evil, know how to give good gifts to your children, how much more will the heavenly Father give the Holy Spirit to those who ask him!"

Luke 11:1–13

At his disciples' request Our Lord shared a prayer which would become the pattern for all our prayer.

We are present at the giving of a priceless gift. The disciples ask Jesus to teach them to pray, and his reply becomes the prayer for all Christians.

"Father." All through his ministry Jesus pleaded for an intimacy between humanity and God. He was determined to instill in us that genuine faith is far more than worship, far more than upholding a historic tradition, and far more than belief in a set of propositions about the nature of the universe and the meaning of human life. It encompasses all these things but it is more. For Our Lord it is above all else possessing a relationship with God. Jesus felt that this relationship was so intimate that he encouraged those around him to use an extraordinarily familiar word for God. That word is, in Jesus' language, *Abba*. We can get some idea how startling this was to his listeners when we realize that the English equivalents are terms such as Pop and Dad!

"Hallowed be your name." Jesus saw that such familiarity deepened God's majesty for us, not diminished it. To believe in God is to become aware of the quality we call holiness or "hallowedness." To believe in God as holy is to believe that life is holy. To experience life as holy is to escape the temptation to reduce life to "just" this or "just" that.

"Give us each day our daily bread." With seven simple words Our Lord has us express our essential dependence. However great our human achievement may be, the simple truth is that we are dependent on the whole interlocked fabric of creation.

"Forgive us our sins." This is the only petition in the prayer that is conditional. Being able to forgive goes hand in hand with being able to receive forgiveness. One cannot happen without the other.

"Do not bring us to the time of trial." Another version of this petition says "Do not bring us to the test." Each is a very natural and human prayer which we should never feel guilty about saying. It was Our Lord's in the garden of Gethsemane.

Having given us the gift of this prayer, a pattern for all prayer, Our Lord continues in the rest of this passage to emphasize God's generosity. That is the Good News for this week.

Sunday between 31 July and 6 August

¹³Someone in the crowd said to him, "Teacher, tell my brother to divide the family inheritance with me." ¹⁴But he said to him, "Friend, who set me to be a judge or arbitrator over you?" ¹⁵And he said to them, "Take care! Be on your guard against all kinds of greed; for one's life does not consist in the abundance of possessions." ¹⁶Then he told them a parable: "The land of a rich man produced abundantly. ¹⁷And he thought to himself, 'What should I do, for I have no place to store my crops?' ¹⁸Then he said, 'I will do this: I will pull down my barns and build larger ones, and there I will store all my grain and my goods. ¹⁹And I will say to my soul, 'Soul, you have ample goods laid up for many years; relax, eat, drink, be merry.' ²⁰But God said to him, 'You fool! This very night your life is being demanded of you. And the things you have prepared, whose will they be?' ²¹So it is with those who store up treasures for themselves but are not rich toward God."

Luke 12:13–21

To have possessions, even great possessions, is quite legitimate. To make them the ultimate focus of life is fatal.

Jesus' constant response to people was a desire to get to the deeper levels which lie beneath the surface. He always tried to take people back to the motivations behind the actions. Behind such things as murder and violence he would point to the anger in us which causes thse things.

In this passage someone asks Jesus to help in the settling of an estate. Jesus refuses. He points out that the issue is not merely the division of the estate, it is also the deep unacknowledged feelings of covetousness. These feelings are clearly revealed by the way the request is made for a referee.

There is another interesting nuance here. The person making the request wants Jesus as an ally to do what they either cannot or do not want to do themselves. Incidentally, Martha in Bethany tried to use Jesus the same way to order her sister to help her. Jesus never responds to such manipulations. He always places the responsibility back where it belongs.

"One's life does not consist in the abundance of possessions." We can easily dismiss this as a kind of motherhood statement, but we need to look at it because our culture has constantly misunderstood this insight of Our Lord. Jesus is not condemning possessions: he is condemning the illusion that possessions can give ultimate meaning to our lives. Neither is Jesus saying that possessions are somehow evil. He is saying that as long as possessions are regarded as things given to us to be used and directed responsibly and compassionately, there is no problem.

The story that follows illustrates these principles. There is nothing wrong with the rich man being rich. There is nothing wrong with his building barns, even bigger barns. Such actions by any farmer or landowner can be very responsible. The trouble begins when we transfer from these reasonable actions to the illusion they can bring. Economic well-being and spiritual well-being do not follow one from the other. The former is important and desirable and quite legitimate. The one thing it must not become is of ultimate value in a human life. That is the Good News for this week.

Sunday between 7 and 13 August

³²"Do not be afraid, little flock, for it is your Father's good pleasure to give you the kingdom. ³³Sell your possessions, and give alms. Make purses for yourselves that do not wear out, an unfailing treasure in heaven, where no thief comes near and no moth destroys. ³⁴For where your treasure is, there your heart will be also. ³⁵Be dressed for action and have your lamps lit; ³⁶be like those who are waiting for their master to return from the wedding banquet, so that they may open the door for him as soon as he comes and knocks. ³⁷Blessed are those slaves whom the master finds alert when he comes; truly I tell you, he will fasten his belt and have them sit down to eat, and he will come and serve them. ³⁸If he comes during the middle of the night, or near dawn, and finds them so, blessed are those slaves. ³⁹But know this: if the owner of the house had known at what hour the thief was coming, he would not have let his house be broken into. ⁴⁰You also must be ready, for the Son of Man is coming at an unexpected hour."

Luke 12:32–40

If we live as men and women who seek the outline of the kingdom of God in our lives, we live compassionately and expectantly.

Jesus is looking around at the circle of those listening to him. As well as his immediate disciples, there are perhaps other men and women drawn to this man and his dream of the kingdom of God. If so they are right to be drawn to it because it will continue to occupy the dreams of men and women until the end of time. In fact it will not only occupy their dreams but it will also call forth commitment and self-sacrifice from many. They will try their utmost to bring into their own society and time even a tiny facet of this kingdom of peace and justice of which Jesus speaks.

''Do not be afraid, little flock.'' Realizing their vulner-ability, Jesus reminds his disciples that power does not always depend upon great legions. A person can taste the kingdom in his or her own life. It depends on the value sys-tem by which we live, the priorities in our lives, the ulti-mate treasure.

''Sell your possessions, and give alms.'' Someone said that Jesus is asking us whether we have riches or riches have us. He is asking us to prove to him by the way we use riches that we really do possess them rather than they us. To return to Our Lord's dream of the kingdom of God, he is saying that if we are prepared to use our possessions responsibly and compassionately, we can taste the vision of personal life and of human solidarity which he offers us in that concept.

''Be dressed for action and have your lamps lit.'' Peo-ple who have been captured by the dream of the kingdom of God live with a sense of expectation. To them history is more than the ongoing pattern of human decision and human action. To them society is the domain of God's action, and they expect to see traces of God's activity.

''Blessed are those slaves whom the master finds alert when he comes.'' Jesus often voiced this thought; it was very important for those who would follow his way. His image here is of slaves who wait for a bridegroom to come home. It was essential for them to be ready the instant the master arrived. Our Lord is demanding that we live always in the expectation of his coming into our lives at any time. Any moment, any situation, any encounter, any challenge, any seemingly ordinary task can be an opportunity for us to serve him. That is the Good News for this week.

Sunday between 14 and 20 August

49"I came to bring fire to the earth and how I wish it were already kindled! 50I have a baptism with which to be baptized, and what stress I am under until it is completed! 51Do you think that I have come to bring peace to the earth? No, I tell you, but rather division! 52From now on five in one household will be divided, three against two and two against three; 53they will be divided: father against son and son against father, mother against daughter and daughter against mother, mother-in-law against her daughter-in-law and daughter-in-law against mother-in-law.'' 54He also said to the crowds, ''When you see a cloud rising in the west, you immediately say, 'It is going to rain'; and so it happens. 55And when you see the south wind blowing, you say, 'There will be scorching heat'; and it happens. 56You hypocrites! You know how to interpret the appearance of earth and sky, but why do you not know how to interpret the present time?''

Luke 12:49–56

Jesus warns his listeners that following him may involve difficult choices, and he warns his society that a just and humane future calls for deep changes.

All through Jesus' ministry there is a sense of premonition. Our Lord was living out nothing less than an alternate way of being a human being in the world! It is obvious that he had no illusions about the dangers he was courting. That alternate way was what he called the kingdom of God and the values of that kingdom were diametrically opposed to those of the society around him, and will be diametrically opposed to the values of any society we have so far devised.

Human empires are not built on giving alms, turning the other cheek, and praying for one's enemies!

Sometimes Our Lord makes no effort to hide that sense of premonition, the feeling that certain collisions are inevitable and they might as well be named and faced. His disciples, on the other hand, seem incapable of accepting the possibilities.

"I came to bring fire to the earth. . . . I have a baptism with which to be baptized." There is intense frustration in these words. Jesus seems deeply troubled at the antagonism to his vision of the kingdom of God, yet, at the same time, to accept the inevitability of its clashing with everything in the life of his time. Even close personal relationships will be deeply divided by his vision. Jesus then moves to another issue. People don't seem to be able to see that the kind of society they are in cannot be sustained: it is headed for tragedy. They are like a man who doesn't realize his case is so weak he had better settle out of court! The society ought to reform itself and not wait for the harsh judgement of the future.

How can all this speak to us? The vision of a kingdom of peace and justice divides us even as Christians. Some people in church life see any social and political activity in Our Lord's name as invalid. Others see it as the only valid Christian task. In society as a whole some people see the vision of peace and justice as less important than the development of wealth, whatever the human cost. In ecological issues many, to use Jesus' phrase, refuse to "interpret the present time" in spite of obvious indications of disaster. As our society moves toward future judgement, as do the two litigants in Jesus' parable, we would do well to settle out of court while we can. Change and reform now, in case the judgement of the future be exceedingly harsh. That is the Good News for this week.

Sunday between 21 and 27 August

²²Jesus went through one town and village after another, teaching as he made his way to Jerusalem. ²³Someone asked him, "Lord, will only a few be saved?" He said to them, ²⁴"Strive to enter through the narrow door; for many, I tell you, will try to enter and will not be able. ²⁵When once the owner of the house has got up and shut the door, and you begin to stand outside and to knock at the door, saying, 'Lord, open to us,' then in reply he will say to you, 'I do not know where you come from.' ²⁶Then you will begin to say, 'We ate and drank with you, and you taught in our streets.' ²⁷But he will say, 'I do not know where you come from; go away from me, all you evildoers!' ²⁸There will be weeping and gnashing of teeth when you see Abraham and Isaac and Jacob and all the prophets in the kingdom of God, and you yourselves thrown out. ²⁹Then people will come from east and west, from north and south, and will eat in the kingdom of God. ³⁰Indeed, some are last who will be first, and some are first who will be last."

Luke 13:22–30

God never ceases to call us, but as life goes on, our capacity to hear God's call and to respond diminishes. We are responsible for making the choices which can avoid this result.

Jesus has come to realize that the forces uppermost in his country's religion and its politics are not prepared to accept the radical demands of his vision. We look at this passage to hear not only what it said to Jesus' own time, but also what it says to us today.

''When once the owner of the house has . . . shut the door.'' Once again Jesus uses the image of the returning master of a house to make his point. In terms of that moment in his own life Jesus is saying that what he stands for and who he is will be recognized too late by some people. It says to every age that life presents certain moments and opportunities which do not come again.

Jesus always emphasized two things about God and human life which seem contradictory but must be held in balance. God is both lover and judge of our humanity. God is the one who seeks us and forgives us. But God expects and demands response. God asks that we make choices, seeing our lives as finally accountable to that power above and beyond the self — that power being God. This power is shown in images such as the householder returning and shutting the door. There comes a time in life when the opportunity has been lost, not because God took it from us but because we have distanced ourselves by our own choices.

''Some are last who will be first, and some are first who will be last.'' These are classic words of Jesus' vision of the kingdom of God. As always the values expressed confront the values we take for granted in society. When Pilate stood before Jesus and asked Our Lord if he was a king, Our Lord said that his kingdom was not of this world. Too often that has been taken to mean that Christian faith should not be involved in the affairs of this world, that it is entirely apart. The truth is that the kingdom of God confronts and judges all human affairs and all human institutions and their values. This very much includes the church itself, which is equally judged by Jesus' vision of the kingdom. The truth is that much of what is first for us is last in the kingdom of God. It would shock and appal us if we could only know the extent of that truth! That is the Good News for this week.

Sunday between 28 August and 3 September

[1]On one occasion when Jesus was going to the house of a leader of the Pharisees to eat a meal on the sabbath, they were watching him closely. [7]When he noticed how the guests chose the places of honor, he told them a parable. [8]"When you are invited by someone to a wedding banquet, do not sit down at the place of honor, in case someone more distinguished than you has been invited by your host; [9]and the host who invited both of you may come and say to you, 'Give this person your place,' and then in disgrce you would start to take the lowest place. [10]But when you are invited, go and sit down at the lowest place, so that when your host comes, he may say to you, 'Friend, move up higher'; then you will be honored in the presence of all who sit at the table with you. [11]For all who exalt themselves will be humbled, and those who humble themselves will be exalted." [12]He said also to the one who had invited him "When you give a luncheon or a dinner, do not invite your friends or your brothers or your relatives or rich neighbors, in case they may invite you in return, and you would be repaid. [13]But when you give a banquet, invite the poor, the crippled, the lame, and the blind. [14]And you will be blessed, because they cannot repay you, for you will be repaid at the resurrection of the righteous."

Luke 14:1, 7–14

Jesus challenges the assumed superiority of those around him at a banquet. The same Jesus as risen Lord challenges us to reconsider the society and world we have helped to form.

It was always very dangerous to invite Jesus to dinner. He had a facility for disturbing the occasion with some extremely insightful comments! However we should not be under any illusion about the motivations of most of those who did invite him to dinner. On occasions, such as this one, the intention was not to honour Jesus but to discredit him before people who could do him great harm if they chose. Luke puts this motive very subtly in five chilling words: "They were watching him closely."

"He noticed how the guests chose the places of honour." As Jesus watched the arrival of the other guests, he saw a seemingly simple thing that said volumes about all that he felt himself to be struggling to change. It was an attitude deeply ingrained in these people, affecting every facet of their lives, their religion, their national life, their behaviour towards others, their relationship to God. Perhaps the only single word that described all this was "self-righteousness." Jesus saw that for these people life centred around themselves, their sense of importance, their superiority to others and to other nations. Jesus realized that their sense of national superiority was taking them toward a fearful catastrophe, and their sense of superiority over other people was destroying their souls.

Because of this realization Jesus tells this parable. The parable is far more effective than an impassioned condemnatory speech in showing these people the terrible reality they are living. At the end comes another expression of Jesus' vision of the kingdom of God. As we might expect, it is totally opposed to the reality in this room. It is in fact a re-stating of the first becoming last and the last first.

There follows a plea from Jesus to those around him to consider even for a moment a different value system.

Once again he presents it in story form, offering a new vision of this very supper which would welcome the poor and the outcast.

The power of all this for us is that Our Lord stands in the great banquet hall of the contemporary, developed world. He questions its sense of superiority, and he pleads that it consider the formation of a world economic order which would at least begin to bridge the gulf between rich and poor. That is the Good News for this week.

Sunday between 4 and 10 September

²⁵Now large crowds were traveling with him; and he turned and said to them, ''Whoever comes to me and does not hate father and mother, wife and children, brothers and sisters, yes, and even life itself, cannot be my disciple. ²⁷Whoever does not carry the cross and follow me cannot be my disciple. ²⁸For which of you, intending to build a tower, does not first sit down and estimate the cost, to see whether he has enough to complete it? ²⁹Otherwise, when he has laid a foundation and is not able to finish, all who see it will begin to ridicule him, ³⁰saying, 'This fellow began to build and was not able to finish.' ³¹Or what king, going out to wage war against another king, will not sit down first and consider whether he is able with ten thousand to oppose the one who comes against him with twenty thousand? ³²If he cannot, then, while the other is still far away, he sends a delegation and asks for the terms of peace. ³³So therefore, none of you can become my disciple if you do not give up all your possessions.

Luke 14:25–33

Jesus calls for ultimate commitment, but, as Our Lord, he accepts the commitment we bring, and offers us grace so that it may grow.

Every step we take with Jesus at this stage in his ministry seems to bring us into harsher and harsher circumstances. His tone gets grimmer. There is an irony about this which Luke gets across in the first five words of this passage. He says that ''large crowds were travelling with him.'' The agony for Jesus is his increasing realization that these hordes of men and women are simply not able to comprehend the vision which he offers. A further irony is that those among the crowds who are able to comprehend it have no intention of accepting it because it threatens their own well-being and their positions and power in society.

"Whoever comes to me and does not hate." To hear that passage even after many centuries is to be chilled by its harshness. It is a terrifying sentence. Down through history, and frequently in recent decades, it has been twisted by exclusive sects to sever the relationships between young people and their families. Our Lord is not saying any such thing. We begin to get at the meaning of this statement when he comes to the phrase, "even life itself."

This is a time in our Bible reading when we must be aware that such exaggerated language was a cultural commonplace in Jesus' society. We can hear this exaggeration in the impassioned political exchanges of Middle Eastern life today. If we go further down the passage to verse 33 we find the heart of Jesus' meaning. His demand for ultimate discipleship is that a man or woman "give up all." What Our Lord is pleading for is that to follow him is to offer our lives to him with singlemindedness and deep commitment. To have a religion that is a mildly diverting weekend hobby is not following Our Lord. Shopping for churches we decide to like or dislike is not following Our Lord. Having an intellectual interest in theology is not following Our Lord. These things are in their own way admirable but they are not what Jesus meant when he said to people, "Follow me."

"Whoever does not carry the cross [v 27]. . . . estimate the cost [v 28] . . . consider whether he is able [v. 31]." The decision to follow Jesus Christ is one of ultimate significance in a human life. Very few of us can respond to the call of Our Lord on the level that some great souls have done. To "renounce all" in a literal way is a fearful thing and is possible only for some. That is precisely why we know these men and women as great souls or saints, both in the past and in our own time. But we decide to follow at the level at which we can and Our Lord accepts us. That is the Good News for this week.

Sunday between 11 and 17 September

¹Now all the tax collectors and sinners were coming near to listen to him. ²And the Pharisees and the scribes were grumbling and saying, "This fellow welcomes sinners and eats with them." ³So he told them this parable: ⁴"Which one of you, having a hundred sheep and losing one of them, does not leave the ninety-nine in the wilderness and go after the one that is lost until he finds it? ⁵When he has found it, he lays it on his shoulders and rejoices. ⁶And when he comes home, he calls together his friends and neighbors, saying to them, 'Rejoice with me, for I have found my sheep that was lost.' ⁷Just so, I tell you, there will be more joy in heaven over one sinner who repents than over ninety-nine righteous persons who need no repentance. ⁸Or what woman having ten silver coins, if she loses one of them, does not light a lamp, sweep the house, and search carefully until she finds it? ⁹When she has found it, she calls together her friends and neighbors, saying, 'Rejoice with me, for I have found the coin that I had lost.' ¹⁰Just so, I tell you, there is joy in the presence of the angels of God over one sinner who repents."

Luke 15:1–10

The degree to which a Christian congregation can become a community of hospitality and outreach is the degree to which it is obeying its Lord.

In the early centuries Christian communities really were communities, places where one could get help, support, friendship, particularly in the big cities of the eastern Mediterranean. Some say that this was the biggest factor

131

in the emergence of Christianity as the religion of the later Roman empire.

This view is not given merely to begin a history lesson. Today we are very conscious of the same need. Our cities are places of deep and widespread loneliness among many people longing for friendship and support. Every Christian congregation needs to be sensitive to this longing and to insure that its life is a welcoming one, not merely to those whom it considers to be its own familiar supporters but to those who come to it seeking community. On any given Sunday that may well be a family newly transferred to the city from another, a person going through crisis who tries the church in his or her great need, a person who may be giving the church another chance after having left many years ago, or people who have for some reason found another Christian tradition unable to serve their need. Each situation is a kind of lostness. The moment we say that word we realize that we have made the connection with the two stories which Jesus tells in this chapter.

"The tax collectors and sinners were coming near to listen to him." These are the people in that long-ago society who felt themselves to be outsiders. On the other hand, the Pharisees, whom Luke shows as resenting Jesus' mixing with the outsiders, were very much on the inside. Luke's image of two mutually wary groups demonstrates another demand that is made of congregational life in today's city. How do urban congregations reach out beyond themselves in ways that are not patronizing and even insulting? How do we support people without making demands on them, at least initially, to conform to congregational life and its many responsibilities?

There is a searching for lost things. A shepherd goes after the sheep which is lost; a woman sweeps diligently until she finds the coin. In congregational life we should not merely wait for needs to appear on our doorstep and then respond to them out of a sense of duty. There should also be a searching for ways in which the resources of the congregation can reach out into the lostness to which Luke refers. When we are prepared to reach in this way we are obeying Our Lord. That is the Good News for this week.

Sunday between 18 and 24 September

[1]Then Jesus said to the disciples, ''There was a rich man who had a manager, and charges were brought to him that this man was squandering his property. [2]So he summoned him and said to him, 'What is this that I hear about you? Give me an accounting of your management, because you cannot be my manager any longer.' [3]Then the manager said to himself, 'What will I do, now that my master is taking the position away from me? I am not strong enough to dig, and I am ashamed to beg. [4]I have decided what to do so that, when I am dismissed as manager, people may welcome me into their homes.' [5]So, summoning his master's debtors one by one, he asked the first, 'How much do you owe my master?' [6]He answered, 'A hundred jugs of olive oil.' He said to him, 'Take your bill, sit down quickly, and make it fifty.' [7]Then he asked another, 'And how much do you owe?' He replied, 'A hundred containers of wheat.' He said to him, 'Take your bill and make it eighty.' [8]And his master commended the dishonest manager because he had acted shrewdly; for the children of this age are more shrewd in dealing with their own generation than are the children of light. [9]And I tell you, make friends for yourselves by means of dishonest wealth so that when it is gone, they may welcome you into the eternal homes. [10]Whoever is faithful in a very little is faithful also in much; and whoever is dishonest in a very little is dishonest also in much. [11]If then you have not been faithful with the dishonest wealth, who will entrust to you the true riches? [12]And if you have not been faithful with what belongs to another, who will give you what is your own? [13]No slave can serve two masters; for a slave will either hate the one and love the other, or be devoted to the one and despise the other. You cannot serve God and wealth.''   *Luke 16:1–13*

Jesus asks that we invest the same energy in our relationship with God that we invest in our personal affairs.

Jesus often outraged his listeners. He would say things that seemed to fly in the teeth of all reality, and advocate things that seemed to offend all their ideas of religious propriety. Jesus was determined to say something so startling that it would penetrate the layers of resistance waiting to block it.

This story is a first-class example. All over Galilee there were great estates run by a manager, — often, but not always, a Greek. The manager was very powerful and in a position of great trust. Therefore, when one was found to be fiddling with the books it was very serious indeed.

Jesus' story is of one such manager. The story may well have been based on a real incident known to his listeners. The master asks for the accounts, and the manager is caught red-handed. But he is resourceful. He rushes around doing deals with his master's customers, deals which will benefit them and therefore make them kindly disposed to him when he comes looking for a job. Thus he survives after being fired. Up to that point it is just an interesting story on human ingenuity. But then Jesus says, "the master commended the dishonest manager because he had acted shrewdly."

The listening crowd must have gasped. Normally the manager would end up in prison. But, as always, Jesus is portraying the nature of God, and applying the attitudes and values of the kingdom of God. What is the most important issue here when we look from God's point of view?

Here is a man faced with a serious situation. Instead of remaining passive he puts every ounce of his intelligence and ingenuity and energy into dealing with the crisis. Jesus now asks us to apply these standards to our spiritual lives, to our relationship with God. Jesus asks that we invest in our spiritual journey those things we invest in the other parts of our life journey. Think of the energy we put into our financial affairs, into our quest for promotion in an organization, into the upbringing of our children. What Jesus is demanding is that we make that investment in spiritual things. That is the Good News for this week.

Sunday between 25 September and 1 October

19"There was a rich man who was dressed in purple and fine linen and who feasted sumptuously every day. 20And at his gate lay a poor man named Lazarus, covered with sores, 21who longed to satisfy his hunger with what fell from the rich man's table; even the dogs would come and lick his sores. 22The poor man died and was carried away by the angels to be with Abraham. The rich man also died and was buried. 23In Hades, where he was being tormented, he looked up and saw Abraham far away with Lazarus by his side. 24He called out, 'Father Abraham, have mercy on me, and send Lazarus to dip the tip of his finger in water and cool my tongue; for I am in agony in these flames.' 25But Abraham said, 'Child, remember that during your lifetime you received your good things, and Lazarus in like manner evil things; but now he is comforted here, and you are in agony. 26Besides all this, between you and us a great chasm has been fixed, so that those who might want to pass from here to you cannot do so, and no one can cross from there to us.' 27He said, 'Then, father, I beg you to send him to my father's house — 28for I have five brothers — that he may warn them, so that they will not also come into this place of torment.' 29Abraham replied, 'They have Moses and the prophets; they should listen to them.' 30He said, 'No, father Abraham; but if someone goes to them from the dead, they will repent.' 31He said to him, 'If they do not listen to Moses and the prophets, neither will they be convinced even if someone rises from the dead.' "

Luke 16:19–31

How do we deal with our physical and tangible possessions? How do we deal with our spiritual gifts? Jesus
requires an answer.

All through this chapter of Luke's Gospel Our Lord is talking about us and our possessions. He says again and again
that this is one of the most important relationships in our
lives, and that we will be judged largely on the way we have
dealt with it.

He has also been saying that possessions can be both
outer and inner. Our relationship to our outer possessions,
from which we take so much pleasure, is only an outward
sign of our relationship with our inner possessions, our
spiritual riches. We can be very rich outwardly and very
poor inwardly. We can be poor outwardly and rich
inwardly. We can sometimes be rich both outwardly and
inwardly, but only if we are prepared to be good stewards
of our riches before God.

The chapter ends with Jesus telling the story of the rich
man and Lazarus. On the surface it is a simple and straightforward story, and we can take a moral lesson from it about
the uses of riches. But it has other levels of meaning, most
certainly to the men and women of Jesus' time and nation.
To them he was presenting the rich man as an image of
themselves, rich and comfortable, but irresponsible and
without compassion for others. On another level Jesus was
questioning his countrymen's use of their spiritual riches.
They claimed a special relationship with God, but how was
this spirituality seen in their actions?

"Between you and us there is a great chasm." It is not
that Lazarus would not go to help, he cannot go. The division is too great, and it is too late. Again Jesus is emphasizing the way judgement takes place in human life. We judge
ourselves by making our own choices and living the consequences. When, in the story, the rich man beseeches Lazarus at least to go to his still-living brothers, the answer he
gets is a terrible one. They have placed themselves beyond

reach, and cannot be made to hear. The terrible truth is that we can by our own patterns and choices place ourselves out of the reach of God. That will certainly not be God's wish for us, but it will nevertheless take place. We are free beings, free to make moral decisions. There is of course always a way back, but only we can choose to take it. All our lives Our Lord offers us grace to help us to choose his kingship rather than that of the tyrant in each one of us which we know as the Self. That is the Good News for this week.

Sunday between 2 and 8 October

[5]The apostles said to the Lord, "Increase our faith!" [6]The Lord replied, "If you had faith the size of a mustard seed, you could say to this mulberry tree, 'Be uprooted and planted in the sea, and it would obey you. [7]Who among you would say to your slave who has just come in from plowing or tending sheep in the field, 'Come here at once and take your place at the table'? [8]Would you not rather say to him, 'Prepare supper for me, put on your apron and serve me while I eat and drink; later you may eat and drink'? [9]Do you thank the slave for doing what was commanded? [10]So you also, when you have done all that you were ordered to do, say, 'We are worthless slaves; we have done only what we ought to have done!' "

Luke 17:5–10

To be human is to experience a struggle for faith.

One of the fascinating facts about the forming of the New Testament is that there existed a lost book in which someone had collected many of the sayings of Jesus. This book circulated before any of the Gospels, and at least two of the Gospel writers, Matthew and Luke, used it. Because the book is lost, and because it was used as a resource by the Gospel writers, scholars have labelled it *Q*, which is the first letter of the German word for a source.

The verses of this passage are from that lost book, sayings of Jesus, saved for us by Luke, which the early followers remembered and thought about. Probably they used them for reflection when they met together to share the bread and wine of the eucharist.

The disciples came to their master one day and they said

"Increase our faith." Does it sound familiar? It should, because you and I have often wished that we could do that when our faith was weak, or has left us for a while. Ironically, we may have thought that if only we had been disciples of Jesus in those years, then faith would have been easy. After all, we would have been walking beside the very source of all Christian faith! But obviously, judging from this request, it wasn't like that at all.

What is being taught to us by this remembered incident? Faith is always a struggle. It is something that you and I have to find and nourish for ourselves; it can never be second hand. Even if you have the unimaginable privilege of sharing a boat or a meal or a walk with Jesus of Nazareth, you must still struggle with your faith.

"When you have done all that you were ordered to do." Jesus is telling us that we can never have the illusion that God owes us something. As he often does, he goes to the other extreme and says that, even when we have done everything we should do, we are still in the eyes of God "unprofitable servants." That could be very discouraging if we take it literally. Is Jesus saying to me that even the best and most faithful service I can offer is futile? No. The other side of the picture is that again and again we see Our Lord accept and affirm what we bring to him, however limited our service may be. That is the Good News for this week.

Sunday between 9 and 15 October

[11]On the way to Jerusalem Jesus was going through the region between Samaria and Galilee. [12]As he entered a village, ten lepers approached him. Keeping their distance, [13]they called out, saying, "Jesus, Master, have mercy on us!" [14]When he saw them, he said to them, "Go and show yourselves to the priests." And as they went, they were made clean. [15]Then one of them, when he saw that he was healed, turned back, praising God with a loud voice. [16]He prostrated himself at Jesus' feet and thanked him. And he was a Samaritan. [17]Then Jesus asked, "Were not ten made clean? [18]Was none of them found to return and give praise to God except this foreigner?" [19]Then he said to him, "Get up and go on your way; your faith has made you well."

Luke 17:11–19

We can take Christian faith for granted so easily, and forget the price Our Lord paid that we might have this gift.

We should linger for a moment on the phrase "on the way to Jerusalem." This journey south wasn't just another trip. This time Jesus would never come back; moreover, he knew the dangers that lay ahead. His selflessness is amazing. Again and again on this journey demands are made on him. He is asked to heal. He is asked to give his opinion on this and that. Always he is present for other people. There is no hint of the dread that must have been inside him at the coming crisis.

"Going . . . between Samaria and Galilee." We have noticed previously that Jesus did not avoid Samaria as most travellers of his religion and nationality did. This in itself is an indication of his refusal to build walls and shut people out. All through his ministry he accepts even the absolute outsiders of his society, when it was obvious that he was making enemies by mingling with such people.

Now suddenly he is face to face with a group of lepers. Even the sight of such a group must have made his heart sink. They were total outcasts. The law had stated a precise distance within which a leper was forbidden to approach other human beings, unless they too had the disease. They tended to form colonies on the edge of communities, dreaded by all, fed by those who loved them.

Jesus gives himself to them in healing. Perhaps giving is the best way to express it because on the evidence of the Gospels healing drained him of energy. Healing is never done without cost to the healer.

The lepers left Jesus before they were healed, and only one returned to thank him. Jesus notes that, and also that the one who did return was a Samaritan. Again it is the second-class citizen, from whom little is expected, who comes through with credit. What is this passage saying to us? There is criticism of Jesus' Jewish contemporaries. They took their relationship with God so much for granted that they had forgotten to be grateful for the rich graces of their faith and traditions. The same can be true for Christians. We can take Christian faith for granted so easily, forgetting the grace it gives to our lives, forgetting also the great cost paid by Our Lord to give us this grace. That is the Good News for this week.

Sunday between 16 and 22 October

¹Then Jesus told them a parable about their need to pray always and not to lose heart. ²He said, "In a certain city there was a judge who neither feared God nor had respect for people. ³In that city there was a widow who kept coming to him and saying, 'Grant me justice against my opponent.' ⁴For a while he refused; but later he said to himself, 'Though I have no fear of God and no respect for anyone, ⁵yet because this widow keeps bothering me, I will grant her justice, so that she may not wear me out by continually coming.' " ⁶And the Lord said, "Listen to what the unjust judge says. ⁷And will not God grant justice to his chosen ones who cry to him day and night? Will he delay long in helping them? ⁸I tell you, he will quickly grant justice to them. And yet, when the Son of Man comes, will he find faith on earth?"

Luke 18:1–8

Jesus asks that our praying be constant and steady, not casual and shortlived.

At first this short passage seems to be about prayer. So it is, but there are other levels of meaning. It will help us to understand them if we consider the situation for Christians at the time Luke was writing.

Christians were beginning to taste the unpleasantness of being an unwelcome and misunderstood minority. Many people saw them as a threat to the integrity and the peace of Judaism. There were agonizing rifts even within families. There were fierce confrontations in the synagogue, the worshipping community, where one might have gone since childhood and was now threatening to eject oneself and

144

one's family. In spite of long and frequent prayer that this ghastly unpleasantness would pass, that one would be accepted among one's own again, things were still not changing at the time Luke wrote. They were in fact getting worse. This is what this passage is addressing: the agony of confrontation and division which resisted all their prayers. Into this situation Luke reminds his contemporaries of Jesus' speaking of "Their need to pray always and not to lose heart." As always with scripture, when we have discovered what it said to those who first heard, we have then to hear it speak to ourselves. In Jesus' story a helpless widow has to get the attention of a judge who doesn't really want to have anything to do with her. She achieves her purpose by sheer tenacity. What is being said to us about prayer?

Our Lord is asking us for a similar tenacity. If we want to know why, we might talk with someone who has prayed about something for a very long time. They will tell us that, as time goes by and we continue to go to God in prayer, we become gradually aware of the true nature of what we are praying about. We begin to see the will of God for us in this matter, not in great dramatic flashes of insight but slowly and with deepening recognition.

As time passes and we remain faithful in prayer we find that a strange and wonderful thing begins to take place. We find that instead of losing heart we begin to take heart. We may not be given what we are praying for, but we are given grace to continue our prayer and so to deal with the situation. That is the Good News for this week.

Sunday between 23 and 29 October

⁹He also told this parable to some who trusted in themselves that they were righteous and regarded others with contempt: ¹⁰"Two men went up to the temple to pray, one a Pharisee and the other a tax collector. ¹¹The Pharisee, standing by himself, was praying thus, 'God, I thank you that I am not like other people: thieves, rogues, adulterers, or even like this tax collector. ¹²I fast twice a week; I give a tenth of all my income.' ¹³But the tax collector, standing far off, would not even look up to heaven, but was beating his breast and saying, 'God, be merciful to me, a sinner!' ¹⁴I tell you, this man went down to his home justified rather than the other; for all who exalt themselves will be humbled, but all who humble themselves will be exalted."

Luke 18:9—14

The heart of Christian faith is to know that in ourselves we are as nothing before God, but by God's grace and love we become as everything.

All through the years of his public ministry Jesus battled attitudes among his people which, ironically, grew out of their religious fervour. In modern times we could say that Jesus pitted himself against the dark side of religion, and it cost him his life.

All through the Gospel walk Pharisees, Sadducees, scribes, tax gatherers, publicans. All of them were part of the varied spectrum of Jewish life, but between them were great gulfs of social, religious, and political differences. To be a Pharisee was by no means to be a bad person, but the attitudes of that tradition often appeared snobbish, exclusive, and superior. Above all there was a tremendous emphasis on the external actions and rules of religion. Against such attitudes Jesus maintained again and again that external rules and observances, while not bad in themselves, were secondary. What was most important was inner spirituality. Tax collectors were absolute outsiders and held in supreme contempt because they worked for the occupying power. They might become very rich but they were still outsiders and cordially detested.

Jesus' parable describes a scene between a Pharisee and a tax collector which anyone could have seen daily in the temple area. The Pharisee is a classic of his tradition. He is confident of his place and his moral condition. His weakness is in the way he dismisses others as lesser men. The tax collector may not be a classic representative of his type. Perhaps others chose to be defiantly self-confident, but this man is under no illusions about himself. However, Jesus suggests that in the eyes of God, he, the self-styled sinner, is the more acceptable of the two men.

All through the Gospel this insight offered by Jesus challenges our natural assumptions. Once again Jesus tells us that the single most necessary step on our spiritual journey is to acknowledge our true state before God, to realize that in ourselves we are nothing but by God's love and acceptance and grace we become everything. That is the theme of the story of the prodigal son. It is the theme of the incident where a woman washes Jesus' feet. It is the hard lesson both Peter and Paul had to learn in their different ways. It is the Good News for this week.

Sunday between 30 October and 5 November

¹He entered Jericho and was passing through it. ²A man was there named Zacchaeus; he was a chief tax collector and was rich. ³He was trying to see who Jesus was, but on account of the crowd he could not, because he was short in stature. ⁴So he ran ahead and climbed a sycamore tree to see him, because he was going to pass that way. ⁵When Jesus came to the place, he looked up and said to him, ''Zacchaeus, hurry and come down; for I must stay at your house today.'' ⁶So he hurried down and was happy to welcome him. ⁷All who saw it began to grumble and said, ''He has gone to be the guest of one who is a sinner.'' ⁸Zacchaeus stood there and said to the Lord, ''Look, half of my possessions, Lord, I will give to the poor; and if I have defrauded anyone of anything, I will pay back four times as much.'' ⁹Then Jesus said to him, ''Today salvation has come to this house, because he too is a son of Abraham. ¹⁰For the Son of Man came to seek out and to save the lost.''

Luke 19:1–10

Some people who seem to have everything long for a deeper reality, but it remains elusive. That reality can be found in Our Lord.

Once again we are walking with Jesus on his last journey south from the lake to Jerusalem. He has taken the river valley road which emerges in Jericho and then turns southwest to climb the escarpment to Jerusalem. At every step of the way it seems someone presents him with some need. It is as if people know that time is running out for him and that they must make their approach before it becomes too late.

By this time Jesus' reputation has preceded him. Many

in this busy prosperous town turn out to see him. Among them is a figure who is both pathetic and yet formidable. He is formidable because he has been given great power over this community by the Roman authorities. He is pathetic because his authority has placed him outside the respect or affection of anyone in this town except those few who owe their livelihood to the Roman administration. This man, Zacchaeus, is the gatherer of taxes.

For some reason he is determined to see Jesus. He is "small of stature," as Luke gently puts it. As he tries to see the famous rabbi, the crowd makes it impossible, probably sniggering as they succeed. In desperation Zacchaeus scrambles up a tree. When Jesus stops beneath him, greets him, and suggests dinner, Zacchaeus is ecstatic.

Something happens between the two men that evening that transforms Zacchaeus's life. We now know the reason for his desperation to meet Jesus. Zacchaeus had come to one of those turning points in life that can make all the difference if the right catalyst is present. This time it is, and the man's life is turned around.

Life is full of such moments if we are only sensitive to them. Perhaps one such moment can be shared. The phone rang a few months ago. Could we meet for a chat? I suggested his office downtown. We met. He turned sideways at his desk, looked out the window, and began to talk. I said almost nothing. He told of his good job and high income, his happy marriage and his great kids. He had all these things. There were no problems except one strange thing, the conviction that there must be something more, some meaning, some binding reality that brought it all together. I asked if he would be prepared to meet a few professionals like himself who had formed an early morning group. He did so. With them, around some Bible study and some sharing, a journey has begun. Who knows, perhaps it will be possible to say what Our Lord said as he left Zacchaeus, "Today salvation has come to this house." There are many Zacchaeuses around. That is the Good News for this week.

Sunday between 6 and 12 November

²⁷Some Sadducees, those who say there is no resurrection, came to him ²⁸and asked him a question, "Teacher, Moses wrote for us that if a man's brother dies, leaving a wife but no children, the man shall marry the widow and raise up children for his brother. ²⁹Now there were seven brothers; the first married, and died childless; ³⁰then the second ³¹and the third married her, and so in the same way all seven died childless. ³²Finally the woman also died. ³³In the resurrection, therefore, whose wife will the woman be? For the seven had married her." ³⁴Jesus said to them, "Those who belong to this age marry and are given in marriage; ³⁵but those who are considered worthy of a place in that age and in the resurrection from the dead neither marry nor are given in marriage. ³⁶Indeed they cannot die anymore, because they are like angels and are children of God, being children of the resurrection. ³⁷And the fact that the dead are raised Moses himself showed, in the story about the bush, where he speaks of the Lord as the God of Abraham, the God of Isaac, and the God of Jacob. ³⁸Now he is God not of the dead, but of the living; for to him all of them are alive."

Luke 20:27–38

Our Lord assures us that the dead are raised, and resurrection is a reality.

This whole chapter in Luke's Gospel is full of tension and confrontation for Jesus. The confrontation is not violent shouting but skirmishes with opponents scattered throughout the crowds. Every now and again one of these opponents calls out a question to Our Lord. The question sounds reasonable, but it is always insincere. It is designed to embarrass Jesus or to get him to make a reply which can be used against him in some future examination and trial.

Luke gives a series of incidents which involve all the social elements which opposed Jesus. The chief priests and the scribes are the first, then come the Sadducees. Their question is typical: it is designed to leave Jesus no opportunity of finding a satisfactory response. It is also a crowd pleaser, and we can hear the titters as the highly unlikely eventuality of the woman and her seven successive husbands unfolds.

Jesus' answer is given in terms of the culture and religious beliefs of his day. It is not necessary for us to evaluate his answer. What is obvious from it is that Our Lord was not prepared to be dragged on to such ground for an argument.

His reply is fairly caustic and makes no effort to hide his awareness of the insincerity of the question. But, as always with Our Lord, he makes use of the situation to respond to the reality that lies behind the question. To know what that reality is we have to know something about that society at this particular time in its history.

Luke in verse 27 says of the Sadducees, ''they say there is no resurrection.'' Up to now in Judaism the concept of resurrection had always been in terms of the nation or the people. Israel would always experience resurrection. Only in recent decades had the question of personal resurrection in an after-life come to the fore. It was a symptom of the overall anxiety and sufferings and sense of oppression in Jesus' day that there should be a concern about what was beyond death. The same is true of our own society. A time of immense change and turmoil and threat has sparked an intense interest in the after-life, in near-death experiences, out-of-body episodes, and the like. This is the anxiety Jesus responds to in verse 37. What he says comes across the centuries and speaks to our own anxieties and fears and hopes about life and death. We hear Our Lord assuring us ''that the dead are raised'' and that God ''is not God of the dead, but of the living.'' That is the Good News for this week.

Sunday between 13 and 19 November

⁵When some were speaking about the temple, how it was adorned with beautiful stones and gifts dedicated to God, he said, ⁶''As for these things that you see, the days will come when not one stone will be left upon another; all will be thrown down.'' ⁷They asked him, ''Teacher, when will this be, and what will be the sign that this is about to take place?'' ⁸And he said, ''Beware that you are not led astray; for many will come in my name and say, 'I am he!' and, 'The time is near!' Do not go after them. ⁹When you hear of wars and insurrections, do not be terrified; for these things must take place first, but the end will not follow immediately.'' ¹⁰Then he said to them, ''Nation will rise against nation, and kingdom against kingdom; ¹¹there will be great earthquakes, and in various places famines and plagues; and there will be dreadful portents and great signs from heaven. ¹²But before all this occurs, they will arrest you and persecute you; they will hand you over to synagogues and prisons, and you will be brought before kings and governors because of my name. ¹³This will give you an opportunity to testify. ¹⁴So make up your minds not to prepare your defense in advance; ¹⁵for I will give you words and a wisdom that none of your opponents will be able to withstand or contradict. ¹⁶You will be betrayed even by parents and brothers, by relatives and friends; and they will put some of you to death. ¹⁷You will be hated by all because of my name. ¹⁸But not a hair of your head will perish. ¹⁹By your endurance you will gain your souls.''

Luke 21:5–19

In an age of apocalyptic change and anxiety Our Lord warns us against chasing impossible visions and claims masquerading as his Gospel and presented to us in his name.

This is one of the apocalyptic passages of the Gospel. In Jesus' lifetime this kind of thinking was prevalent. It saw a time of great distress as imminent. Beyond that time there would be a time of transformation according to God's design as the Lord of history. However, the period between the present and that hoped-for transformation would be grim indeed. The significance for us of passages such as this is that a great deal of this kind of thinking is around today. We too are living in an apocalyptic age.

Jesus' remark about the temple (verse 6) was the kind of statement that was to come back to haunt him in his trial. One of the charges against him was his subversive statements about the temple. The irony was that Jesus was perfectly correct. On more than one occasion he made it quite obvious that he thought that unless the various radical policies and attitudes of his country were changed there would be fearful consequences. Within forty years of the crucifixion his worst fears were realized. The temple was utterly destroyed.

We must remember that Luke was writing this passage after the destruction of Jerusalem, and many of the things he mentions were beginning to happen. Many voices were claiming to be inspired political and religious leaders [verse 8]. Some Christians in various parts of the empire were already beginning to encounter persecution of various kinds, some of it from a militant Judaism and a great deal from Roman authorities beginning to be concerned about the new movement. Against this background Luke includes verses 10 to 19.

What, then, does a passage like this say to us today? We have already mentioned that there is a great deal of apocalyptic thinking abroad. Much of it is in the writing and the voices of certain Christian traditions. Charismatic leaders emerge to build media empires, only to fade away again. Claims to be guided and inspired by God are made. Voices claim the ability to prophesy the future. Cults form and break up and reform in other guises. Bizarre religions flourish. All of this is typical of an apocalyptic age. Wise men and women remain faithful to the historic Christian communities which have stood the test of time. In such worshipping communities scripture and sacrament mediate the grace of Our Lord who is "the same yesterday, today, and forever." That is the Good News for this week.

The Last Sunday after Pentecost: the Reign of Christ

⁹When the great crowd of the Jews learned that he was there, they came not only because of Jesus but also to see Lazarus, whom he had raised from the dead. ¹⁰So the chief priests planned to put Lazarus to death as well, ¹¹since it was on account of him that many of the Jews were deserting and were believing in Jesus. ¹²The next day the great crowd that had come to the festival heard that Jesus was coming to Jerusalem. ¹³So they took branches of palm trees and went out to meet him, shouting, "Hosanna! Blessed is the one who comes in the name of the Lord — the King of Israel!" ¹⁴Jesus found a young donkey and sat on it; as it is written: ¹⁵"Do not be afraid, daughter of Zion. Look, your king is coming, sitting on a donkey's colt!" ¹⁶His disciples did not understand these things at first; but when Jesus was glorified, then they remembered that these things had been written of him and had been done to him. ¹⁷So the crowd that had been with him when he called Lazarus out of the tomb and raised him from the dead continued to testify. ¹⁸It was also because they heard that he had performed this sign that the crowd went to meet him. ¹⁹The Pharisees then said to one another, "You see, you can do nothing. Look, the world has gone after him!"

Luke 12:9–19

As Jesus rides into Jerusalem he also rides into the world of our time, as well as into our personal lives, and he demands our response to his claim to be king.

We have been following Jesus on the journey south from the lake in Galilee. We have now arrived on the hillside to the east of Jerusalem, the hill called the Mount of Olives.

155

Jesus knows there is a plot on his life, yet he also knows that the time has come for confrontation. He must make a gesture that challenges the system which he has been so deeply questioning. As he looks at the city on the smaller hills below him he knows that he is seen as a threat by all the network of systems that make up that city and any other society. There really isn't very much room in the world for people who pray for their enemies, turn the other cheek, and suggest that the poor and the meek will inherit the earth! — there never has been, and there never will be! To this day people with visions of a transformed society of peace and justice must, like Jesus, be prepared for some very unpleasant consequences.

Only by this realization will we understand that in a mysterious sense the Gospel drama is being played out in every generation. As we read these verses we see Our Lord preparing to ride into Jerusalem. But Our Lord, crucified and risen and living eternally in history, is always riding into the city of our time. By the term "city" we mean not just our city in a literal sense, but all the systems and organizations and power structures which make up our contemporary urban civilization. Into this powerful and complex system Our Lord rides and claims to be king. What does that statement mean?

Our Lord always spoke of a kingdom. He called it the kingdom of God, and he was referring to a set of values which deeply questioned the values of our political and economic systems. Some Christians get angry when statements like this are made. They feel it is disloyal and subversive and irresponsible to question the very structures by which, if we are honest, we all live. But Christian faith and the Christian church is placed in the sometimes unwelcome and thankless position of having to question the political and economic structures SIMPLY BECAUSE THESE STRUCTURES ARE CONFRONTED BY THE VALUES OF THE KINGDOM OF GOD AS EXPRESSED BY OUR LORD. In fact we are forced to go further, to say that those values of the kingdom of God also confront the structures and the policies and the values of the church itself! There is even one step more we must go as we watch Our Lord ride into Jerusalem. The eternal truth is that he rides into the city of our personal lives and claims to be king there too! That is the Good News for this week.

Other Books by Herbert O'Driscoll

Praying to the Lord of Life: Reflections on the Collects of the Christian Year according to the Book of Alternative Services

A Time for Good News: Reflections on the Gospel for People on the Go Years A, B and C

Child of Peace, Lord of Life: Reflections on the Readings of the Common Lectionary

Year A, Volume 1 (from the First Sunday of Advent to the Fifth Sunday in Lent)

Volume 2 (from the Sunday of the Passion to the Last Sunday after Pentecost)

Year B, Volume 1

Year B, Volume 2

Year C, Volume 1

Year C, Volume 2

A Year of the Lord Reflections of Christian Faith from the Advent of the Christ Child to the Reign of Christ as King

A Certain Life: Contemporary Meditations on the Way of Christ

Portrait of a Woman: Meditations on the Mother of Our Lord

Crossroads: Times of Decision for the People of God

The Sacred Mirror: Meeting God in Scripture

One Man's Journal: Reflections on Contemporary Living

City Priest, City People: One Man's Journal, Book 2

Books on Spirituality

Soft Bodies in a Hard World: Spirituality for the Vulnerable by Charles Davis

Total Health: The Fourth Dimension by George Birtch

From Creation to Resurrection: A Spiritual Journey by Sister Constance Joanna Gefvert

Books on Christian Life

An Open View: Keeping Faith Day by Day by John Bothwell

Taking Risks and Keeping Faith: Changes in the Church by John Bothwell

New Life: Addressing Change in the Church by John Bothwell, John Davis, J.C. Fricker, Sheila and George Grant, Dorothy Gregson, Philip Jefferson, Elizabeth Kilbourn

Gift of Courage: by James Wilkes